CONCRETE UTOPIA

CONCRETE UTOPIA

Looking Back into the Future of Human Rights

WOLFGANG KALECK

Translated by David Youssef

OR Books
New York · London

© 2023 Wolfgang Kaleck

Published by OR Books, New York and London

Visit our website: www.orbooks.com

First printing 2023

Library of Congress Cataloging-in-Publication Data: A catalog record for this book is available from the Library of Congress.

British Library Cataloging-in-Publication Data: A catalog record for this book is available from the British Library.

Typeset by Lapiz Digital.

paperback ISBN 978-1-68219-439-3 • ebook ISBN 978-1-68219-440-9

CONTENTS

"Whatever utopia is, whatever can be imagined as utopia, this is the transformation of the totality . . . what people have lost subjectively in regard to consciousness is very simply the capability to imagine the totality as something that could be completely different."

Even though ". . . all humans deep down, whether they admit this or not, know that it would be possible or it could be different. Not only could they live without hunger and probably without anxiety, but they could also live as free human beings."

". . . then I would say that this is due to the situation compelling people to master the contradiction between the evident possibility of fulfillment and the just as evident impossibility—of fulfillment only in this way, compelling them to identify themselves with this impossibility and to make this impossibility into their own affair."

— Theodor W. Adorno, from "Something's Missing: A Discussion between Ernst Bloch and Theodor W. Adorno on the Contradictions of Utopian Longing" (1964), in *The Utopian Function of Art and Literature: Selected Essays*

Foreword to the English Version

Human Rights in Times of Crisis

This short work was never intended to present a finished concept of the concrete utopia of human rights. Rather, it was meant to provide a glimpse into the ongoing self-reflection of someone grappling with the sometimes hopeful, but mostly grim, realities of human rights work around the world—someone who wonders why human rights discourse is not playing a larger role in the debates about the environmental catastrophe and global pandemic now unfolding before our eyes. Have we not already, for decades, spelled out the meaning and importance of economic and social rights, with the right to water, the right to an unspoiled environment, the right to health? Shouldn't these rights have necessitated an expansion of all health systems across the world, long before and during the pandemic, along with the joint development of a vaccine available to everyone—instead of the prevailing situation of "vaccine-apartheid"?

With both climate change and the pandemic, we are currently witnessing—again—the most vulnerable and marginalized being forced to foot the bill. Don't we need to be even more emphatic in advocating especially for their human rights in light of these circumstances? Shouldn't we be more vocal in countering the predominant narrative that we are all equally affected and "in the same boat"—as if social inequality both within our societies and between them had not increased dramatically during the pandemic?

These striking injustices are rooted in a destructive global economic system and in political decisions in tax, trade, and other spheres of law—and also in the lack of regulation of the activities of corporations—which have been built on the exploitation of people and nature during the last two centuries and which continues to accelerate its ravages. And what about those of us in human rights and civil liberties organizations? Don't we put our energies all too often into particular issues that, while important in their own right, are symptoms and don't touch structural problems? By focusing on our respective regions and specializing in our respective fields, we remain siloed and fragmented, strangely out of touch with the totality of crises, or "polycrisis," if you will.

I asked myself these and other questions in this book and seek to discuss them amongst our community and beyond. For that reason alone, an English version of this book is helpful. English is of course the language of those whose economic metropolises dominate and disfigure the world, but that same English offers a universal tongue that enables us to have a common understanding. I am happy to say that—thanks to OR Books and Colin Robinson—the English-language edition is now available. This book was first published in Germany in the midst of the pandemic in March 2021—when bookstores and public venues were closed. Even before the pandemic, it was not easy for people and organizations from different parts of the world to communicate, let alone actually cooperate. Our living and working conditions could scarcely be more different. Some face civil and criminal lawsuits, financial or fiscal sanctions and, at times, danger to life and limb, while others—in Western Europe and North America—have privileged access to resources, media, and international forums.

The pandemic and the latest push toward digitalization have set us back yet again in our efforts to network and develop a sense of the global scale of the polycrisis, as well as common strategies against it, without obscuring the differences in our thinking, actions, and basic circumstances. Recent realities have made such contrasts even more stark: the Western middle-class human rights activists enjoyed the pandemic deceleration of their lives with good wine and good books, while their salaries and government funding continued to flow and the shocks to their societies were contained. Many others, on the other hand, became more isolated than ever from world events and had to work under precarious conditions in economically fragile societies.

As a result, the rifts between us have widened. The internationalist spirit that fuels our work has been left malnourished, while our sense of global solidarity has suffered from the fact that we couldn't travel or meet as much in person, to simply talk, laugh, eat, drink, argue and, in the end, to embrace the basis of the collective action that is necessary to tackle the excesses of these crises.

The 10th of December of 2023 will mark the 75th anniversary of the Universal Declaration of Human Rights of 1948. The promise in Article 1, "All human beings are born free and equal in dignity and rights," is an expression of hope and, at the same time, a concrete utopia that remains unfulfilled. This essay aims to chronicle the recent history of human rights as a history of struggles led by those who strive for absolute justice and who are never satisfied with what has been achieved thus far, as well as by those who embrace learning how to come to grips with the contradictions of this world. In this respect, the ambivalence of law—as protector of human rights on the one hand and as instrument of domination and governance on the other—continually confronts those of us who are immersed in these struggles, forcing us to navigate a landscape of political pitfalls as we simultaneously look into an abyss of human suffering.

This despair, this rage—indeed sometimes even this helplessness—amid the schizophrenia of our lives must be articulated. These factors constitute an individual, collective, and political challenge for us. If we do not face this challenge, we risk losing the many others who share our view that the world must alter its course: that it is simply wrong that people die of hunger and curable diseases, as well as in massacres or from torture.

We do not need advertising slogans, images, or press releases to applaud us. Instead, we need candid words and the will to live and fight together with others (even virtually, if absolutely necessary). And not just because this is an ethical imperative (which it is) but also because it can be fulfilling for us not to simply watch the suffering of this world impotently on a computer screen and, instead, to intervene against it.

The German Marxist philosopher Ernst Bloch, to whom the concept of a concrete utopia can be traced, describes it as an active process, in which our initial task consists of "determinate negation": the negation of that which merely is, but which has proven to be false. We must therefore begin a critical analysis of today's realities. However, in the spirit of Karl Marx's eleventh thesis on Feuerbach which is still on display in the foyer of Berlin's Humboldt University: "Philosophers have only interpreted the world in various ways; the point is to change it."

But what does this mean in times of polycrisis when the mounting dilemmas we face force us to choose between ugly alternatives? For example, even in times of war, there is no question that the extraction and use of fossil fuels must be stopped as soon as possible. This does not mean, however, that we should simply take what is presented to us, such as the Green New Deal or a green economy, as the only alternative. Rather, a socio-ecological transformation, which also extends beyond our Western societies, requires a global view that takes into equal consideration the interests and needs of all people in all regions of the world. The neocolonial seizure of indigenous territories in Mexico for the construction of wind power plants and the exploitation of lithium deposits in Bolivia, Chile, and Argentina may represent a shift away from fossil fuels, but this does not amount to a just solution for all. That is why, in the discourse on ecological transformation and climate change, the human rights of those who are already heavily impacted by extreme climate events—such as the floods in Pakistan or the ongoing water shortages in the expanding desert regions of Africa—must be strengthened. Moreover, we have to find a position towards the big polluters of air and water in China or Russia. The phenomena of environmental destruction goes beyond western capitalist countries.

This is all the more true in the new geopolitical situation where we find ourselves, where the Western bloc—with the United States on the one side and the Europeans on the other—is posing as the guardian of democracy and human rights. The aggressor Russia and its corrupt, despotic rulers, first and foremost Vladimir Putin, must be sanctioned according to the rules of law: the arrest warrant of the International Criminal Court in The Hague against Putin is thus not at all directed at the wrong person. Russia is not only leading a war of aggression but also committing all kinds of war crimes.

Yet, from the perspective of international law, it must also be remembered that twenty years earlier, in March 2003, the United States and the coalition it led attacked Iraq without legitimacy under international law on the basis of false facts. That war cost hundreds of thousands of people their lives, and thousands were tortured in US and British prisons, while the guilty were never forced to stand trial. However, this failure of the West should not lead to less justice and accountability: it should encourage us all to demand that international standards be applied to all, without double standards. The increasing militarization of our societies and our languages, in addition to the formation of war economies which are accompanied by astounding increases in the cost of arms, must be stopped. The use of these weapons—including the threat of nuclear weapons—will further destroy our world. The resources that would be needed for a socio-ecological transformation of our societies have been mobilized for the expansion of the military.

As regrettable as the authoritarian tendencies in China, Russia, India, Turkey, and the political regression in the United States may be, there is also positive news: Latin America has recently voted for the left once again. To think globally also means to not merely see the negative developments, but to also see the glimmers of hope and flashes of utopian moments, and to follow the example set by people in many places in the world who oppose all the forms of destruction of humans and the natural world that are described in this book.

This year, September 11th is a significant day for many people around the world. Especially in the southern part of the American "double continent," we are once again reminded of how neocolonial thinking and language shape us. When we speak of 9/11 and mean the attacks in Washington and New York, we are at the same time disappropriating Chileans and Latin Americans of the memory of their September 11th, which is the anniversary of General Augusto Pinochet's military coup supported by the United States and its allies 50 years ago.

This 50th anniversary of this coup reminds us that the history of the West after 1945 has never been an unbroken story of unconditional commitment to democracy and human rights around the world. On the contrary, those who claim to be guardians of the rule-based international legal order have never adhered to international law when it conflicts with asserting their own interests, be it in the pursuit of their anti-communist doctrine during the Cold War or, nowadays, in securing raw materials during deals with Saudi Arabia.

However, if we are to activate our historical memory, then let's not only remember the fatal defeats of the left: 2023 will also be the 25th anniversary of the arrest of the same Augusto Pinochet in London in October 1998, on the basis of an arrest warrant issued by the Spanish investigating judge Baltasar Garzón, for the torture of opponents of the regime that he ordered during his dictatorship. This criminal proceeding emerged from exiled Argentine and Chilean communities in Spain and human rights networks around the world. His arrest reverberated throughout Chile and Argentina, where hundreds of military officers have since been convicted, and where those affected by their crimes—along with hundreds of thousands of protesters—are not only campaigning for a reckoning with the past evils of the dictatorship, but also for uprooting the legacies that can be traced back to it: a neoliberal economic system, an authoritarian constitution, and the institutional disfigurement of society, not to mention massive foreign debt.

Times may not have become easier, especially during the last three years, but it has never been easy to stand up for the concrete utopia of human rights. Only through the spirit of global solidarity can the fight for human rights generate the possibility of their enforcement. Generations before us have failed, due to the enormity of the task—but they did it with their heads held high and with a smile on their faces.

Wolfgang Kaleck
Berlin, June 2023

Prologue

This essay was actually supposed to be written in the big city, in New York in early 2020. I wanted to explore whether and how we can take effective legal action against human rights violations with my colleagues there. I wanted to discuss the challenges that lawyers face when coming to terms with colonialism with actual postcolonial theorists. And I wanted to orchestrate creative and legal interventions with artists. Despite our differences, we—my colleagues from leading human rights organizations from the United States, Mexico, Argentina, India, the United Kingdom, and myself—wanted to tighten the networks forged in recent years. Through exchanging ideas and approaches on how to more rigorously address the systemic causes of human rights abuses—such as inequality—we planned to commit ourselves to closer cooperation with each other and with my own organization, the European Center for Constitutional and Human Rights (ECCHR) and its partners.

Travel captivates me. I felt the need to witness the remnants of slavery in the US southern states of Alabama and Mississippi with my own eyes, in particular the National Lynching Memorial in Montgomery, a project initiated by the civil rights lawyer Brian Stevenson. My colleagues in Haiti were going to give me insight into the seemingly never-ending cycle of slavery, debt, economic crisis, natural disaster, and repression, which even the historic moment of the revolution and liberation from colonialism in 1804 could not break.

But, as we are all well aware, things turned out differently in 2020. Travel was hardly possible, which forced me to miss out on the inspiration and stimulation that comes from personal experience and unique encounters. The internationalist spirit of our work is still suffering from this distance.

Ultimately, this essay was not written in the buzzing metropolis but, instead, in the contemplative quiet of Berlin during the first lockdown, as well as in the even more secluded countryside of Brandenburg. I do of course lament the fact that I had to forego the rest of my stay in the US, although without truly wanting to remain in the deserted and unreal New York of March 2020. Like many other members of the metropolitan middle class, I also enjoyed the dramatic slow-down in the pace of life that accompanied the start of the pandemic—which soon gave me the clarity to see just how much this current crisis is connected to what I wanted to write about.

I also of course experienced passing moments of disillusionment and anxiety about the future. But I wasn't overcome by them; instead, I was furious at the political and economic elites of this world who helped ensure that the pandemic became such a disaster in so many places in the world. And little by little, I became increasingly confident in the conviction that not only did other people share this attitude, but also that it was in our hands to go out and change the course of events. I owe this insight to friends like the two Indian human rights lawyers Colin Gonsalves and Kranti.

While I was still enjoying the view of the highline and the factories from my university office in Queens, Colin recounted pogroms against Muslims to me on the phone. He told me about his travels to the Muslim slums of Delhi and how he had attempted to combat the threat of large-scale massacres through legal means, and how he stood by the people. They could not take special precautions against the coronavirus, he shouted, laughing sarcastically: they had enough other problems to contend with that threatened to destroy the lives of many people and the natural world in India.

Just like Dr. Rieux in Albert Camus' *The Plague*, Gonsalves, a winner of the alternative Nobel Prize[1], has spent his entire life grappling with human rights violations so massive in scale as to seem unimaginable to outsiders: colonial injustice, colonial and postcolonial hierarchies, a legal system that has never been decolonized, and caste and class antagonisms as fierce as ever. These conditions were overwhelming to me, and yet so far away at the same time.

Only days later, his associate Kranti told me what damage the completely ill-prepared European-style lockdown in the megacity of Bombay was doing to the dysfunctional state. People searching for work, food, and water were mobbed by the police, driven off the streets with batons,

---

1   Right Livelihood Award, granted by the Swedish Right
     Livelihood Foundation.

beaten and killed. Those who ensure the existence of public life at the risk of their own health for wages that cannot even secure them a living—the so-called "front-line workers"—lacked any protection from the virus.

My friends' organization, Human Rights Law Network, sued the government to force it to provide protective gear for these people by means of expedited court requests, but this initially failed due to the unwillingness and incompetency of Indian judges. Because the judges felt exposed to the virus, they refused to enter the air-conditioned rooms of their workplace in the center of Bombay. The plaintiffs' case was surely not so urgent that it had to be heard immediately. This was a toxic mixture of ignorance, class arrogance, and the failure to value human life that is not only characteristic of Indian history.

It was difficult to hear such stories first-hand, but they also threw my own privilege into relief and helped me to fend off the rampant navel-gazing especially on display in Germany, where notions of solidarity extended no further than to the boundaries of the neighborhood, the city, or the country. My colleagues all over the world and I have had to come to the painful realization that since March 2020, the differences and frictions within and between our societies have become increasingly entrenched, making the conditions of our human rights work even more precarious, as we are forced to persevere within the national borders constructed for us.

This is why the focus here is on global solidarity and not on solidarity in any of its paternalistic guises. At the same time, however, we cannot allow the real danger of paternalism to be used as an excuse by those who prefer to keep their distance from the suffering of others. It remains an invaluable endeavor to cultivate an understanding of the global interconnectedness and complexity of this world, as well as a sensitivity—along the lines of Immanuel Kant—that allows us to feel the injustice at work in other places in the world, wherever we happen to be. And I must add: we need to develop an idea for the unity of struggles in different places across the globe, while simultaneously approaching them from our own individual situations.

From the outside, day-to-day human rights work often appears erratic and lacking in strategy. We often react too late, with insufficient means, powerless in the face of tremendous dangers. Despite—or perhaps because of—these daily pressures, we cannot allow ourselves to avoid critically reflecting on our practice, nor can we allow for theory and practice to be played off against each other.

The purpose here is not to seek out a theory that maps onto practice, nor is it to champion a theoretical ideal that should be practically implemented in the future. The aim here is rather to engage productively with the ambivalences and contradictions of this world, namely, those found within the tension between the "infinity of justice," as Jacques Derrida so vividly put it, and the struggle for rights in the here and now.

This essay is written by someone whose work is situated within this schizophrenic tension, someone who allows himself to reflect on justice in its grand incompleteness, even while he is usually sufficiently occupied with the everyday struggles against injustice. Suffice it to say, there is neither the space here to adequately explore all these problems and questions, nor is this territory already so well-trodden as to be ripe for a finished concept. With this book, I am attempting to offer a glimpse into a continuous, dialectical internal dialogue, in order to promote—hopefully soon, in the coming post-pandemic period—the necessary cross-pollination between actors already engaged with these issues and, moreover, to carry the discussion further out into society.

The following text has set itself the task of cracking open a window onto a very concrete utopia, the concept of human rights, which has proven itself to be tremendously powerful in the past and whose potentials for the future are vast. Invoking a "concrete utopia" in this work's title may seem misleading, as this term is associated with the critical modern philosopher Ernst Bloch, who ultimately anchors his concept as a natural law in terms of the philosophy of history. Yet, such essentialistic theoretical foundations are not available (anymore) for a (legitimation) theory of society today. However, the potentials for a movement of thought and a justification of action that point toward the future—a justification for which Bloch also stands—should be linked together. Through this connection, the transformational potential of human rights can reveal itself and merge with a political theory of human rights.

Currently, the impacts of human rights endeavors are often measured using rather short-term standards:

victory or defeat, just like in football. Reality is compared to ideal conditions, and the latter's failure to appear is proclaimed to be the "endtimes of human rights." Philanthropic sponsors of human rights work impose economistic metrics, while non-governmental organizations send out triumphant press releases. In place of such assessments, I would like to offer an alternative historical and political understanding of human rights work in practice.

A look back at the French and the Haitian Revolutions at the end of the 18th century will illustrate the transformative and utopian potential of human rights. Although conceived initially as a revolution of the propertied male bourgeoisie, it was the women's movement, the Haitian revolutionaries, the workers' movement, and much later the civil rights movement who attached their claims to the declaration of universal human rights. These historical movements have shown us that overcoming the circumstances in which humans are oppressed by other humans can only be achieved through a confrontation with political conditions and with power—and finally, how the seemingly impossible can become real.

Like nothing ever before, the COVID-19 crisis has illuminated just how fraught and complex our world currently is and just how much everything is connected to everything else. The current disaster reveals an intensification and synchronicity of problems that were already percolating within the economic and financial crisis of 2008, the rise of authoritarian tendencies, and the climate crisis.

Nevertheless, the old world as we have come to know it was not all bad. That is why it is crucial here to detect those elements—however fragmentary—of real practice and real actors, and to bring them together, thus allowing a greater whole—a vision—to emerge out of the particular juxtapositions, the seemingly disconnected activities. In this endeavor, I would like to map out some of the areas where it is necessary to fight for human rights—and also where people are actually fighting, even if often under a different flag: against inequality, poverty, racism, the persecution of minorities, repression, and surveillance. There is resistance everywhere. Utopias and even heterotopias are appearing on the horizon.

What role exactly do human rights play in these struggles? Are they, as is commonly understood today, the solution or at least part of the solution? Are they part of a broader strategy of transformation? The modern human rights movement is often thematically compressed into political and civil rights by the Western public while remaining geographically concentrated in the capitals of human rights diplomacy and justice: New York, London, Geneva, and The Hague. The movement deserves constructive criticism.

One mode of intervention that goes beyond reports, studies, and campaigns is legal action. From the arrest of Chilean ex-dictator Augusto Pinochet in London in the fall of 1998, to cases against large transnational corporations, to the collective social and legal struggles in Africa, Asia, and Latin America over the right to water and the right to food, the last 25 years have seen substantial developments, without, however—and this must be addressed here—actually leading to structural change.

Finally, this book will attempt to illuminate what those urgently needed transformational processes in the name of human rights could look like. The focus will center around several different movements that view themselves as alternatives to existing circumstances and are thus already imbued with emergent utopian energies. Committed artists also have an important role to play here: they enable us to grasp the concrete utopian project of human rights on an emotional, as well as a rational, level—attuning us in our actions to the contours of the utopian as we are pulled into utopia's orbit, even as it remains beyond our reach. This aspiration is intended as an antidote to that way of thinking that Zygmunt Baumann has dubbed *retrotopia*, which sees a better future as impossible and therefore turns toward an idealized past. More on this to come.

From Retrotopia to Utopia

The end of history and the angel of history

For the neoliberal economist Milton Friedman, classical liberal philosophy already stood for a free market and a free society, as well as for human rights. With this in mind, it should surprise no one that in his speeches in the year 1990, former US President George H. W. Bush proclaimed the birth of a new world order "of freedom and human rights in every country on earth." This proclamation contributed to the early narratives of human rights discourse that framed human rights as the natural outcome of an evolutionary progress—a progress with which Western liberal democracies believe that their history is imbued. From the perspective of many left-wing and progressive forces—particularly in the Global South—this effectively discredited the concept of human rights, especially after it became instrumentalized in the 1990s and 2000s by certain Western governments and neoconservative ideologues to justify military interventions and regime change.

There was talk of the "end of history," emanating from the end of the Cold War and within Francis Fukuyama's book of the same name. This notion, however, was not really intended to convey that history was coming to an end. It was the triumphalist cry of the victors of the Cold War: "There is no alternative" (TINA), which initially called for deregulation and privatization and then later—after 1989—the adjustment of the political system. With the fall of the Berlin Wall, the totalitarian systems were declared to be defeated and the path toward liberal democracy unimpeded. Once more, history would be written by the victors and by their will to lord over the meaning of progress for as long as possible. For a good while, this undoubtedly worked in the 1990s and 2000s.

Today, even Fukuyama sees democracy as under threat by authoritarian regimes and populist governments like Donald Trump's presidency in the US, as well as by inequality. Few still share his belief from that time that the ultimate purpose of historical progress—to reach a state of complete freedom and reason—had almost been fulfilled.

On the contrary, as Zygmunt Baumann describes in *Retrotopia* (one of his last books), our contemporary moment can be seen as a phase of nostalgia shaped by the promise of rebuilding an imagined ideal of homeland that stands at the center of influential ideologies and nationalist revivals which we are now encountering all over the world. Because many people cannot imagine a new and better world beyond the one in which we live today, today's visions no longer draw their energy from the future, Baumann argues, but rather from "the lost/robbed/orphaned, in any case undead past."

Baumann recalls Walter Benjamin's "Theses on the Philosophy of History." Taking as his point of departure a painting by Paul Klee which the philosopher had purchased in 1921, Benjamin described Klee's image of the angel of history:

> A Klee painting named "Angelus Novus" shows an angel looking as though he is about to move away from something he is fixedly contemplating. His eyes are staring, his mouth is open, his wings are spread. This is how one pictures the angel of history. His face is turned toward the past. Where we perceive a chain of events, he sees one single catastrophe which keeps piling wreckage upon wreckage and hurls it in front of his feet. The angel would like to stay, awaken the dead, and make whole what has been smashed. But a storm is blowing from Paradise; it has got caught in his wings with such violence that the angel can no longer close them. This storm irresistibly propels him into the future to which his back is turned, while the pile of debris before him grows skyward. This storm is what we call progress.

According to Benjamin, "The past carries with it a temporal index by which it is referred to redemption. There is a secret agreement between past generations and the present one. Our coming was expected on earth. Like every generation that preceded us, we have been endowed with a *weak* Messianic power, a power to which the past has a claim." What is called for here is not blind faith in historical progress—which both the social democratic and communist movements shared during Benjamin's time—but, rather, the staging of a revolutionary political process.

Baumann claims that in the current age, the angel of history now gazes terrified into the future while drifting inexorably in the direction of the past. We live "in an age of disruptions and discrepancies, an age in which everything—or almost everything—may happen, while nothing—or almost—can be undertaken with self-assurance and with the certainty of seeing it through." In order to confront the prevailing fear of the future, we must convince the angel of history to once again turn itself around.

Walter Benjamin always insisted upon a conscious attunement to past struggles for freedom and equality and, in particular, the remembrance of the vanquished. With his demand on future generations "...to complete what has been withheld from us" and "to save what has failed," he thus espouses a leftist conception of history that sees itself within a continuum of past and future leftist struggles for freedom and equality. An awareness and energy for the substance of human rights can be siphoned from this tension.

The French philosopher Enzo Traverso proposes a leftist, melancholic vision of history. Sealed definitively in 1989, the demise of "real socialism"—something which Traverso himself also viewed critically—shattered the dialectic between past and future. Past events and defeats could thus no longer become inscribed within a historical consciousness— which, in this respect, is also contrary to a Marxist conception of history—so that they may be projected into the future, as a kind of strategic memory of past struggles, as well as a future-oriented memory.

According to the historian Reinhardt Koselleck, the present furnishes the past with meaning. The latter, he said, offers the actors of history "a reservoir of memory and experience, which enables them to formulate their expectations." Koselleck pointed out that while in the short term "...history is made...by the victors, historical gains in knowledge stem in the long run from the vanquished."

For Walter Benjamin, it is thus about "seizing a memory as it flashes up at a moment of danger." We live in a time that forms a dialectical connection between an unfinished past and a utopian future, "in which the past fuses together, like lightning, with the present to form a constellation."

What Benjamin describes here seems unthinkable today. Like him, we live in an unjust world—sometimes even a dystopian one—and we wish for this to change; yet too seldom do we trust in our ability to make this happen. However, the French Revolution and the Haitian Revolution show that historical caesuras are possible—and that such desired and necessary events do in fact occur, breaking with the previous course of history.

Unthinkable histories

I would like to broaden the historical perspective on human rights and recall two potent historical events: the French Revolution with its "Declaration of the Rights of Man and the Citizen" of August 1789, which for many people marks the birth of universal human rights, and the Haitian Revolution, which is often still forgotten to this day.

On August 26, 1789, the French National Assembly proclaimed the "Declaration of the Rights of Man and the

Citizen." The Declaration still has a lasting effect, though these rights have not yet been fully realized even in our current day and age. Historians and others still argue about how such a declaration actually came into being. Human rights thus exemplify contingency, the openness of history, as well as hope, precisely because no one could have predicted this event, which was so significant in world history—even if the first signs of it, within the philosophical works of the Enlightenment or the novels of the era, were already evident.

The Declaration's seventeen articles stated, among other things, that "Men are born and remain free and equal in rights." (Art. 1) and that the "The aim of every political association is the preservation of the natural and imprescriptible rights of Man. These rights are Liberty, Property, Safety and Resistance to Oppression." (Art. 2). In addition, the freedom of religion, freedom of expression, and fundamental judicial rights were also declared.

But declared did not mean realized, not by a long shot—especially not for all the groups that were excluded by the male, propertied creators of the great human rights declarations in the United States of America in 1776 and the French Revolution in 1789. Nevertheless, as US historian Lynn Hunt lucidly explains in her book *Inventing Human Rights*, completely new political perspectives and avenues opened up for those who were previously excluded. Henceforth, Protestants and Jews, women and black Haitians, the fourth estate and, later, the labor movement, all now had a normative template to buttress their political struggles.

During the French Revolution, it became clear that while those who drafted the declarations made use of the language of universal human rights, they did not have the inclusion of groups other than a white, male propertied middle class in mind in practice. This meant, even at the beginning of the revolution, that children, prisoners, foreigners, people without property, slaves, "free blacks," religious minorities, Jews, and especially women were essentially excluded from the purview of rights (the right to have rights)—an oft-criticized contradiction.

Once proclaimed, however, universal human rights developed a momentum of their own. According to Hunt, after the declarations, the use of these forms of legal terminology increased dramatically. People demanded their rights, and state institutions made reference to the law, limiting the omnipotence of the sovereign. One example was the way that the long process of abolishing torture and cruel corporal punishment came to an end with the decision of the National Assembly in October 1791.

Of course, this declaration did not supply all the answers to all questions, which too must be a lesson for us today. Rights, once articulated, raise new questions—questions that were neither asked at the time, nor even askable beforehand.

Hunt recognized that the Declaration was only the first step in a political process that continues today. There was no end to it because new demands were always being made. Thus, within two years of 1789, religious minorities were able to obtain almost all of their political rights: Protestants achieved this in December 1789, followed by

Jews in the south of France in January 1790, and then Jews in the eastern part of the country in 1791, each invoking the fact that the same rights had previously been granted to other groups. The floodgates, once opened, could not be closed.

Women's rights, as well, were suddenly on the table. As recently as the beginning of the French Revolution, women's equality was unthinkable. But the "Declaration of the Rights of Man and the Citizen" also animated women, above all the author and activist Olympe de Gouges, leading them to demand their rights from that point onward. Her "Declaration of the Rights of Women and the Female Citizen" begins with these striking words: "Man, are you capable of being just? It is a woman who poses the question; you will not deprive her of that right at least. Tell me, what gives you sovereign empire to oppress my sex?"

This speech by de Gouges admittedly fell on deaf ears during the French Revolution. She herself was executed as a counter-revolutionary. But the discussion had now commenced, opening an unforeseeable, uncharted space for debate, for conflict, and for change. The promise of equal rights for women, Hunt argued, could be rejected and suppressed or simply left unfulfilled, but it would still live on.

The entire process of the liberation of slaves and the abolition of slavery—especially in the case of the Haitian Revolution—also demonstrates this.

If the French revolutionaries, and the US revolutionaries before them, had been serious about their talk of universal human rights, they would have had to immediately abolish slavery of their own accord. But the protagonists of both states and both slaveholding societies did not want to face this consequence. As Haitian anthropologist Michel-Rolph Trouillot vividly puts it: "The Haitian Revolution was the ultimate test to the universalist pretensions of both the French and the American revolutions. And they both failed..."

After the indigenous Caribbean people had been practically wiped out in Spanish-colonized Hispaniola, slaves abducted from Africa were forced to grow tobacco, coffee, cotton, and, above all, sugar under the most inhumane conditions in what then became the French colony of Saint-Domingue.

Many died, as more and more slaves were brought to the colony, where the population had reached an estimated 800,000 people. A revolt against these conditions seemed impossible, as a French colonist wrote to France as late as 1790 in the vernacular of the time: "'There is no movement among our Negroes...They don't even think of it. They are very tranquil and obedient.'" Trouillot reflects: "Indeed, the contention that enslaved Africans and their descendants could not envision freedom—let alone formulate strategies for gaining and securing such freedom—was based not so much on empirical evidence as on an ontology, an implicit organization of the world and its inhabitants."

Prior to 1789, only the so-called "free blacks," freed former slaves and their descendants who were allowed to own land and hold slaves, had organized themselves. Inspired by the revolutionary events in France and their principles, they demanded equal rights for themselves without wanting to free their own slaves. While smaller uprisings in 1790 did not succeed, in 1791 the slaves rose up and defeated the French army in several battles and won territorial sovereignty.

In France, people refused to accept that black people—who were generally regarded as lacking in maturity and sophistication—were liberating themselves and so they reacted incredulously and belatedly. The debates in the West "dealt with the impossible only after that impossible had become fact," Trouillot says, "and even then, the facts were not always accepted as such." In 1792, the National Assembly in Paris granted equal rights to all inhabitants of its colonies, regardless of skin color, but rescinded that decision later that same year. In the National Convention in 1794, Deputy Levasseur again made a motion to proclaim the freedom of all black people, justifying his claim by saying: "While drafting the constitution of the French people, we neglected the unfortunate men of color." Later, the decision was made to abolish slavery.

Within a short time, what Michel-Rolph Trouillot called "unthinkable history" continued to develop. Under the leadership of Toussaint Louverture—whose parents had been deported from Benin to work in the sugar cane fields—the black population decisively defeated the French army in 1799 in a difficult war with significant losses. Toussaint demanded "the recognition of the absolute principle that no man, white, black or red, may be the property of his fellow man." They are free today "because we are the stronger ones."

After shifting developments on the battlefront, Toussaint Louverture, who was by now the governor, was captured by Napoleonic troops in 1802, taken to France, and executed there. But the colony could not be recaptured and Napoleon's troops were finally defeated in 1803. The revolutionaries declared the state independent on January 1, 1804 and renamed it Haiti, the first independent state in Latin and Central America.

France recognized Haiti only much later and also successfully demanded reparations to compensate former plantation owners—a debt burden that, along with the ongoing interference of other world powers—as well as a Haitian government that was as despotic as it was corrupt—strangled the Haitian economy well into the 20th century.

For many slaves and their organizations, the Haitian Revolution served as a model and an impetus to revolt and fight for their self-liberation, as can be read in *The Many-Headed Hydra: Sailors, Slaves, Commoners and the Hidden History of the Revolutionary Atlantic* by Peter Linebaugh and Marcus Rediker. Trouillot states that the Western world, on the other hand, was under the illusion that "what happened is what must have happened." Because the self-liberation of the slaves still seemed unthinkable to them, and because it contradicted the image that the West had of itself and of others, this history remained largely concealed for quite some time. For him, this concealment and silence around the Haitian Revolution is merely another chapter within the West's generally accepted description of its own global domination.

"It is part of the history of the West and it is likely to persist, even in attenuated form, as long as the history of the West is not retold in ways that bring forward the perspective of the world," Trouillot claims.

For us contemporaries, it is therefore necessary to tell this story over and over again in order to rewrite universal world history—as well as to generate hope for the realization of human rights.

Back in France and further along in the course of the French Revolution, the rights of workers and the lifting of the ban on associations and strikes in "Le Chapelier Law" were discussed and demanded in the craftsmen's and workers' clubs. The fourth estate—the proletariat—and others were also to be given their rights in the "Declaration of the Rights of Man and the Citizen," a document advanced by Maximilien Robespierre in April 1793, insofar as Article 21 stipulated that: "Society owes maintenance to unfortunate citizens, either procuring work for them work or in providing the means of existence for those who are unable to labor." Furthermore, Gracchus Babeuf's "Manifesto of Equals" explicitly called for real equality beyond the formal equality of the 1789 Declaration, as well as for common ownership of the earth and its fruits.

In the 19th century, the nascent labor movement invoked the French Revolution and the "Declaration of the Rights of Man and the Citizen." Formal equality as an abstract principle and the political equality of male citizens with the nobility and the clergy already constituted immense historical progress. Subsequently, those who were still oppressed even after 1789—such as religious minorities, women, blacks, and workers—invoked the principle of equality until, according to legal philosopher Christoph Menke, "it finally concerned nothing less than 'real' or 'de facto' equality."

The revolution of human rights

Taking the French human rights declaration of 1789 as a starting point, how might this political process be described? Menke and his colleague Francesca Raimondi see the revolution and human rights as having "in an inner systematic connection," which they explore within their notion of the "revolution of human rights":

> Human rights are not merely basic normative claims, whose assertion may in some or many cases necessitate or justify an overthrow of existing political, social and economic conditions. Rather, human rights are the instructions for a form of politics that is much more revolutionary because its practice consists in a constant undermining, displacement, overthrow of relations – including those once judged to be in the name of human rights.

For them, the human rights declaration "stands for the moment" when "the old order has been dismissed and a new one has been demanded, without having yet been established." Human rights therefore constitute "a pretext to further arrogate to oneself the right (for example, by those who have not yet spoken) to protest against institutionalized violence, and indeed always to do so in new and different ways." Francesca Raimondi writes:

The...limited nature of the human rights declaration, which is evident precisely in the fact that it is merely a declaration, is reinterpreted in the revolutionary reading as an anticipation directed toward future critique and political struggles. In this respect, the human rights declaration is precisely not limited but, rather, contains a double presumption, because it establishes principles and rights that are (politically) not yet realized, and in so doing attributes this act to someone who also does not yet exist – the free human being.

For Raimondi and Menke, human rights stand for the "principle of a different politics"; thus, they argue for a political conception of human rights and not for a natural law/moral conception of them, which would assign to politics the role of merely implementing rights that had already been "pre-politically" established. In this sense, human rights declarations are, as per Raimondi, "a political act that sets natural law against an old political-legal order and establishes it as the foundation of a fundamentally new political constitution."

For Christoph Menke, therefore, "the revolutionary process...[does not possess] a logic by which action is governed in its goal and course by a reason that precedes it but, rather, one of an adventure, an attempt, or a permanent revolt; the logic of a positing that is also annulled by the very thing it produces." The application of these concepts to human rights practice is markedly different from the approaches of human rights actors today, which to me is quite exciting.

But isn't the notion of revolution too contrived, on the one hand, and too stale, on the other? The human rights revolution must certainly not be about simply replacing the old regime with a new one by way of a political overthrow and only replacing the elites. Rather, the decisive factor is to develop a politics directed toward freedom and equality, which must be free of authoritarian tendencies and arrive instead at its own forms and content. In the course of doing so, this politics should draw inspiration from history and its interpretations.

Not a distant island: Bloch's concrete utopia

In his work, the philosopher Ernst Bloch developed the concept of the "concrete utopia." With this, he wanted to show the real potential for fundamental social change, which differentiates itself from abstract utopias. Concrete utopia, according to Bloch, is not the "coloring-in" of a picture already hanging on the wall—a fool's fantasy or some saccharine dream floating above us. "After all, the substance of utopia is ultimately nothing if it does not refer to the Now." For him, utopia functions "only for the sake of the present which is to be attained." "Not only if we travel there, but *in that* we travel there the island utopia arises out of the sea of the possible," which is precisely the occasion of utopia becoming concrete. For Bloch, "the present rules together with the horizon within it, which is the horizon of the future, and which gives to the flow of the present specific space, the space of new, feasibly better present."

Concrete utopia then consists of a structure of thought that points toward the future, rejecting what is currently wrong and containing a well-founded critique of present conditions, using historical experience to think our way into the future.

Following Bloch in this respect, the Senegalese philosopher Felwine Sarr also considers it necessary to "look at history as a space of possibilities, of new constellations and new compositions, and to imagine the possible, beyond the real." At the beginning of the coronavirus pandemic, Sarr claimed that the "real," as we have come to know it, is in the process of disintegration. He argues that we should resist the temptation to quickly patch it back together and restore the old normality that is so toxic for so many people. Instead, we should accelerate this collapse and thus open up a path toward social transformation.

The concrete utopia describes an active process in which our initial task is the "determinate negation"—of that which merely is, but has proven to be false—within a critical analysis of contemporary realities. This echoes Karl Marx's eleventh thesis on Feuerbach, which is still enshrined in the foyer of the Humboldt University: "Philosophers have only *interpreted* the world in various ways; the point is to *change* it."

Building on this premise, creating a concrete utopia is a matter of discerning the incipient vibrations within the present so that they may be amplified, while at the same time conceiving the spaces of the "real" and making them into reality by thinking and acting together with others. We must desire to do this—and plunge ourselves into the hazardous terrain of current and imminent confrontations, even if we do not know what is coming. Nothing can be foreseen.

This metaphor helps us grasp the ambivalences of critical human rights theory and practice, the difference between the short-term progress (or even regression) in the realm of human rights and the perpetual failure to address more systemic problems.

But how can human rights as a concrete utopia be realized? Interventions can serve as a tool for this, as they strive toward two goals on multiple levels: those which are oriented toward the whole, i.e., undoing societal injustice on a grand scale, and those that have more particular, concrete objectives.

Just to clear up any misunderstandings—especially among lawyers: it deserves to be briefly stated that the conventional concept of intervention originates from the domestic and foreign policy context and means to interfere in the affairs of another state or influence such affairs through actions that target an influential person. In the meantime, the term has been adopted in the fields of education, medicine, and psychology, as well as by artists who, for example, engage in interventions into existing social contexts through artistic works and performances in cultural settings or public spaces. Because of its two-fold meaning, the term also makes sense within the legal and human rights context—especially in its interplay with the notion of concrete utopia.

Interventions also become conceivable and possible when manifesting the latter, even though their successes are uncertain and cannot be calculated in advance. According to sociologist Helmut Willke, "the momentum of the system can cause an intervention's direction and impact to weaken, stay at standstill, or even be reversed." This is why he speaks of the improbability of successful interventions.

His conclusion becomes all the more valid when taking different kinds of interventions into consideration. Result-oriented interventions can be characterized as having clear objectives, for example, in the area of public health or conflict resolution. The more process-oriented interventions, on the other hand, often entail interfering with the dynamics of highly complex social systems in a non-trivial way, which is why such interventions aim to initiate a process.

By means of such interventions, cascading events can be triggered, but the extent to which their impacts endure is another matter. The success / failure, victory / defeat paradigm—which is so fatally simplified in political and social life just as much as in human rights work—could be overcome if those involved in process-oriented interventions were aware that unanticipated events or irritations may follow their efforts. When the aim of an intervention, however, consists of developing new approaches, new structures, and new patterns of behavior, further actions are needed that lead to the opening up of new courses of action and the establishment of new decision-making processes in the long run.

Of course, the conditions for claiming that a human rights intervention is possible need to be defined in more detail. Admittedly, the current consensus seems to be that in law, as in art, the claim and assertion of the term itself should alone suffice. In contrast to that assumption, the action of the intervening party must be suitable for triggering an effect of a certain significance, meaning, or strength—and the intervenor must intend for this to happen. Human rights intervenors are thus required to engage with existing political power relations, to desire to change them concretely and not just simply to formulate the corresponding appeals. I will come back to interventions, at least briefly, both in conjunction with the legal actions to be addressed later on and with artistic endeavors in the human rights context. Both areas constitute important terrains of the struggle for human rights, as they both exhibit—in spite of their embeddedness within systemic structures—a relative independence and autonomy.

I would first like to show in the next chapter where the utopian content of human rights might be found, as well as what the reality of human rights institutions and norms created after 1945 has been.

The Concrete Utopia of Human Rights and the Reality after 1945

"All human beings are born free and equal in dignity and rights." This is how briefly and succinctly the concrete utopia of human rights is declared in the first sentence of Article 1 of the "Universal Declaration of Human Rights" of December 10, 1948. This article is utopian because it describes a condition for all people in the world to strive for. It is readily apparent, however, that in reality other conditions prevail. It is not foreseeable if and when the claim that all human beings are born free and equal in rights will become a reality.

With the "Universal Declaration of Human Rights," a programmatic document was created after the Second World War that was far ahead of the political circumstances of its time and that today still contains useful potential in various respects. In reaction to the "acts of barbarism" committed by the National Socialists, as it was so formulated in the preamble, it represented a consensus of diverse ideological currents of the time—which, incidentally, was achieved through the active participation not only of important figures in the West, such as Eleanor Roosevelt or René Cassin, but also of non-governmental organizations such as the American Jewish Committee and of diplomats of the Third World (albeit without the participation of large sectors of the world's population who still lived in the colonies).

It is often overlooked that in addition to the important individual basic rights to life, freedom, freedom of movement, and the prohibition of slavery and torture, the Declaration also contained economic, social, and cultural human rights, of which large portions of humanity to this day can only dream, such as the right to social security, the right to work and equal pay, as well as the rights of trade unions and the right to education.

For roughly two decades, the human rights declaration remained merely a recommendation, without any actual, underlying international treaty planned at the time to enforce it. There were neither legally binding norms to be upheld, nor institutions and courts to enforce them. According to a widely held interpretation, the victorious Allied Powers had sought to create a "charter of the great powers." Other states did not want to be bound legally, among them also the European colonial powers, as they feared that this would obstruct their own policy of fighting against anti-colonial efforts.

The victorious powers of World War II held the Nuremberg trials of Nazi war criminals with the claim that they were establishing a new global legal order. But at the same time, they were violating the freshly established rights at every turn in the context of the embattled decolonization movements. Great Britain and France suppressed the anti-colonial freedom movements in Kenya, Algeria, Indochina, and Africa through asymmetrical wars using all means at their disposal, which also included torture, mass arrests and massacres, as did the smaller colonial powers, such as Netherlands in Indonesia, Belgium in Congo, and Portugal in Southern Africa. The British colonial minister Arthur Creech Jones epitomized this attitude when he described the Charter in 1949 as a "source of embarrassment."

Just as Michel-Rolph Trouillot viewed the Haitian Revolution as the ultimate test of the universalist claims of both the French and American Revolutions, Ralph Bunche, one of the architects of the UN Charter, saw the colonial question as a test of the ability of the post-war order to implement the ideals and principles for which the victorious powers of World War II—and with them millions of African and Asian soldiers from the colonies—had fought.

Despite the lack of legally binding authority, the United States and the Soviet Union, along with the decolonized states that had become independent, repeatedly invoked human rights in UN forums, at least during the first decades after World War II. Human rights and the accusations of class segregation and discrimination in the US, Australia, and South Africa—on the one hand—and the forced labor and political prisoners within the Soviet Union, on the other, shaped the ideological battlegrounds of Cold War. This was less about helping the political prisoners in the Soviet Union or Black people in the US to achieve their rights than it was about morally and ideologically discrediting one's respective opponent in the Cold War.

Otherwise, the Soviet Union and China broke practically every law against their own citizens: namely, with the enormous camp systems containing millions of people and the oppression of national minorities.

The US, in turn, was responsible for dozens of overt and covert *coups d'état* against democratically elected governments, such as Jacobo Árbenz in Guatemala, Juan Bosch in the Dominican Republic, Mohammad Mossadegh in Iran, and Salvador Allende in Chile in 1973, and has been directly or indirectly involved in decades of repression by military governments and militaries in southern Latin America and Central America.

Because of the reluctance of these powers and, above all, because of the stalling maneuvers of the colonial powers Great Britain and France, the process of constitutionalization was delayed. Much later than was intended, in December 1966, the two major covenants for civil and political rights ("Civil Covenant") and for economic, social and cultural rights ("Social Covenant") were adopted by the UN General Assembly, finally officially going into effect in 1976. This was followed by numerous conventions with specific prohibitions against discrimination, such as those on racial discrimination (1965), discrimination against women (1979), as well as the Convention on the Rights of the Child of 1989 and the Convention on the Rights of Persons with Disabilities of 2006. In the field of international humanitarian law and international criminal law, the Geneva Conventions—together with additional protocols such as the Genocide Convention of 1948 and the UN Convention against Torture of 1984— are worthy of mention. Internationally and independently staffed treaty committees monitor compliance with and implementation of these covenants. In some cases, individual complaints can also be submitted to these committees. Step by step, an increasingly dense system of human rights protections has been established.

These steps, from the programmatic recommendations of the 1948 "Universal Declaration of Human Rights" to the international juridical rights established in the covenants of 1966 and thereafter, only took place gradually.

Human rights became more international, and utopia became more concrete. Extending beyond the minimal consensus of rights of defense vis-à-vis the state, the human rights of different generations became enshrined. These were (after or alongside the first generation of classical political and civil rights), the economic, social, and cultural rights of the second generation, followed by the third generation of collective rights—formulated in vague manner that is not justiciable—including, among others, the right to development, which is quite significant for the majority of UN states.

In the course of the struggles for decolonization, Afro-Asian states organized one of the most important historical events of the last century, the Bandung Conference in Indonesia in 1955, whose final communiqué also emphasized human rights as a foundational principle of the new world order, in conjunction with the right of peoples to self-determination. Human rights were being violated by continued colonial rule and apartheid. The Algerian liberation movement FLN placed this issue at the center of its diplomatic and political efforts, including before the UN.

On this basis, the expanding coalition within the Third World, united in the Non-Aligned Movement and the Group of 77, then called for a "New World Economic Order," which would include a system to ensure fair trade and fair commodity prices, as well as to regulate investment and transnational corporations. These efforts resulted in UN Resolution 1514 in 1960, one of the most important, which guaranteed the right of peoples to self-determination. Because of the strong Afro-Asian bloc, the UN, and—along with it—human rights, played a significant role in world politics, especially during the years of decolonization. The superpowers continued to pursue policies aligned with their self-interest. Nevertheless, utopian moments occurred again and again within the sphere of the UN, such as the UN General Assembly Declaration of 1974, which aimed at improving global justice and the welfare of people exploited by colonialism by narrowing the gap between industrialized and developing countries. The preamble to the 1986 UN General Assembly resolution describes the right to development as "a comprehensive economic, social, cultural and political process, which aims at the constant improvement of the well-being of the entire population and of all individuals on the basis of their active, free and meaningful participation in development and in the fair distribution of benefits resulting therefrom." The call in Article 3 of the same document for a new world economic order "based on sovereign equality, interdependence, mutual interest and cooperation among all States" appears equally utopian.

The industrialized countries ultimately put the brakes on these initiatives. The BRICS (Brazil-Russia-India-China-South Africa) countries have themselves recently profited from the regularities of the global economy that were once under attack. Many of the problems identified at the time, however, persist. One of the most important postcolonial critics, Antony Anghie, also notes as an important difference that "the earlier campaign was waged in the name of sovereignty and the present one in the name of the cosmopolitan cause of human rights."

The final declaration of the Second World Conference on Human Rights in Vienna in 1993 upheld both the universality and indivisibility of human rights, not least of which because of the expansion of the catalog of human rights. At the same conference, the Office of the High Commissioner for Human Rights was created, reporting directly to the UN Secretary-General, one of the many new institutions under the umbrella of the United Nations to coordinate the latter's human rights work.

The role of the Security Council has also changed in recent decades. Its role is no longer limited to preventing interstate conflicts. In the past, this limitation led the Council to shy away from interfering in the internal affairs of a state. Now, the most serious human rights violations are also considered a "threat to the peace, breach of the peace" under Article 39 of the UN Charter.

But the standard of judgment is disputed among the various blocs. Some see themselves in the tradition of humanitarian universalism, since the interventions of the 18th and 19th centuries concerned the British Empire's self-interested fight against the slave trade. Others, such as Russia, China, and many states of the South, feared that the West—in historical continuity with the "civilizing missions" of the colonial era and the numerous interventions of the post-war period—would abuse the accusation of human rights violations as a legitimization of potentially convenient regime changes.

In 2005, for example, the UN General Assembly adopted the so-called "Responsibility to Protect/R2P" in the event of the most serious human rights violations and breaches of international humanitarian law by a state against its own population. However, the UN did not play a major role due to the above-mentioned reservations held by many states.

For example, in the case of the devastating civil war in Syria that began in 2011, Russia and China vetoed all of the more far-reaching Security Council decisions. They are rightly criticized for this. However, this criticism remains as superficial as the current complaint about the erosion of international law. Often, the focus is exclusively on the posture of authoritarian rulers and regimes, which do deserve harsh criticism. What is ignored is that Western states also contributed to such eroding tendencies, for example, with counterterrorism, in which the same methods were used as in the suppression of the anti-colonial movements. President George W. Bush weakened international law with his decisions to systematically torture terrorism suspects in Guantánamo and elsewhere, and then once again when he invaded Iraq in 2003 to overthrow Saddam Hussein's regime against established international norms. The Europeans did not stand in the way of this development.

In the last two decades, opportunities to strengthen multilateralism and to develop truly universal standards have been wasted. In 2011, for example, the UN Security Council—with the participation of China and Russia—explicitly emphasized the Libyan state's responsibility to protect its own population in the accordance with the tenets of the R2P and referred the case of Libya to the International Criminal Court in The Hague. Subsequently, however, this decision was used by Western states to legitimize the violent overthrow of ruler Muammar al-Gaddafi. In view of such a validation of their reservations, no one should be surprised by the return of Russia and China to their old blockade position in the case of Syria, with its well-known fatal consequences.

The UN Human Rights Council also has a rather mixed track record, because there are states that have been accused of serious human rights violations among its elected members. Nevertheless, each member state in the Council must now regularly submit to a periodic review of its human rights situation conducted by the other states—a procedure that national and international NGOs use to compile and publicize crucial reports.

Many documents of the UN General Assembly and its subsidiary bodies read like the quintessence of the most committed reports and recommendations on each respective topic. The establishment of independent individuals in special working groups and their deployment as UN special rapporteurs on topics such as torture or extreme poverty, as well as on individual countries such as South Africa and Myanmar, has contributed in particular to this.

For quite some time now, (human rights) diplomats are not the only ones found in the corridors of the UN in Geneva and New York. Rather, a porous multilateral scene of representatives of the UN and its member states has formed—along with academics, experts, NGOs, and lobbyists—a scene which often provides visibility for certain problems and affected groups.

The human rights protection systems in Europe and the Americas—namely, the two human rights courts in Strasbourg and San José in Costa Rica—were developed from the 1970s onwards and played important roles in numerous intra- and interstate conflicts. The current crisis of legitimacy is unsurprising, as the Inter-American Court lacks both the financial resources to continue its work adequately and also lacks an enforcement mechanism vis-à-vis member states.

In Europe, key rule-of-law principles have been relativized in recent years primarily along two lines of reasoning: the terrorism paradigm and the migration paradigm, which often overlap.

Russia and Turkey are the two states most frequently ruled against by the European Court of Human Rights. The violations of the conventions as a result of the Chechen conflicts, the armed conflicts in the Kurdish areas in Turkey, and the current situation in Ukraine or after the coup in Turkey in 2016 are especially dramatic. Russia therefore wants the Russian Constitutional Court to advise in the future on how the decisions of the European Court are to be implemented in Russia, instead of recognizing the binding legal force of these judgments.

The national populist discourse is making itself visible not only among the notorious violators of the law from the states in the Council of Europe. The populist demand for "Swiss law instead of foreign judges" even became the subject of an—ultimately unsuccessful—Swiss referendum in 2018. Also, even in Western states governed by the rule of law, politicians look aslant at election results and—especially in times of crisis—undermine legal guarantees such as the protection of minorities and the principle of a fair trial. France, for example, declared a state of emergency after terrorist attacks by lone perpetrators in Nice and suspended fundamental rights not only for terrorism suspects but also for unpopular demonstrators at the Paris climate summit. In the United Kingdom, government politicians questioned the competence of the Strasbourg court, especially in military conflicts, because the

UK had been convicted several times of torture and other abuses against prisoners of war in Iraq.

The current system of European migration—in which the central European states of Germany and France rely on the EU border states of Spain, Italy, and Greece to bear the entire burden of migration and also enable them to adopt unlawful methods in constructing their border facilities—is in conflict with numerous rights. Both virtual and actual barriers have been extended and moved out beyond Europe's borders since the early 2000s. Moroccan authorities, for example, have increasingly prevented refugees and migrants from even reaching the border with Spain.

Numerous migration prevention agreements between European and African states, personnel support, and technical deployments have brought the external European border far beyond the EU's territorial demarcation lines. In West Africa, the externalization of the European border regime restricts freedom of movement and has reactivated borders that were constructed during colonial times.

Human rights violations and the death of people are tolerated when blocking escape routes. When confronting the death toll on the Mediterranean, political scientist Nikita Dhawan wrote: "Once again we are witnessing a crisis in European ambitions to be the guarantor of global justice, human rights, and democracy. The disenchantment with Europe as a consequence of colonialism and the Holocaust is once again coming into focus."

Thus, the utopian aspiration of Article 1 of the 1948 "Universal Declaration of Human Rights" has only been partially realized, and multilateralism is experiencing a crisis. The UN remains weak and recently has even had funding problems. The organization has partially opened itself up to civil society, yet is ever-still dependent on states and their interests.

Accordingly, states cannot be released from their own fundamental responsibility for human rights. However, a detailed and comparative analysis of the situation in individual states would require a more profound and more detailed analysis than can be provided here. For this reason, in the following chapters I would like to focus on the disputes over human rights at the international and transnational level, along with the growing tendencies toward rampant authoritarianism and the repression of civil society actors, as well as the resistance to these phenomena. Many states, along with right-wing populist and nationalist politicians and parties, subordinate law and human rights to their political goals for the sake of a diffuse "common or national good." As a counterweight to this development, great attention must be given to civil society actors in addition to supranational institutions and states. First, however, we must take a brief look at the big picture: the current pandemic crisis.

2

Bringing the Big Picture into View: These Crises Don't Come Out of Nowhere

We are accustomed to breaking down complex problems into manageable units. There's of course nothing wrong with a passion for detail and solid facts—in fact, we can't do anything without them. But in keeping with the spirit of the worldwide Fridays for Future demonstrations, we can no longer afford to avoid the obvious clustering of problems and the complexity of the situation. The big picture must be brought into focus.

The pandemic became a global disaster due to the culmination of many negative developments in recent times. It has often been the case that only the privileged of this world have had access to the health care system. For example, even in the 1990s, tens of thousands of people in Africa died of AIDS because they had no access to antiretroviral drugs. Long before Bill Gates warned of a possible highly contagious virus in a 2014 speech, sociologist and historian Mike Davis in 2005 had already addressed this very danger, which could potentially wreak global havoc. The encroachment upon natural habitats and the resulting proximity between humans and animals, the developments within the agricultural industry—especially the use of antibiotics and other drugs in animal breeding—has led to new mutations of viruses. According to experts fifteen years ago, in order to avert this danger, a concerted global effort to develop a vaccine and a functional global health system would be necessary. In 2012, an expert commission from the World Health Organization had already called for the establishment of supranational patent pools for joint research into how to combat global health threats such as pandemics. This initiative was thwarted by the powerful states.

In recent decades, by means of neoliberal austerity programs, we have instead seen a politically imposed dismantling of such capacities that are accessible to all people within the general health care system. In many places, these capacities are being privatized, excluding large sectors of the world's population from functioning health care. Meanwhile, other, more lucrative treatments—such as beauty enhancements and anti-aging medicine—are flourishing in the rich countries.

Not everyone is in the same boat: some are vacationing through the crisis on luxury yachts, while many of us in Western Europe and North America find ourselves on reasonably safe ships. But even in this part of the world, many are just adrift on makeshift rafts or swimming in the tides, fighting for survival at every turn. Certainly, rich and prominent individuals have also become infected, and some have died. But Boris Johnson and Donald Trump have been cared for around the clock by teams of doctors, while the residents of old people's homes in Bergamo and Madrid—along with refugees and prison inmates—have been left to their own fate, as have the poor in the United States, not to mention those in the favelas of Brazil or the slums of Bombay.

To say that the crisis is an opportunity would be in poor taste. Yet to understand it as an eye-opener can be helpful for the development of concrete utopias. The cultivation of hope that is truly well-founded—as Ernst Bloch understood it—presupposes the analysis and critique of the existing state of affairs in the world and the determinate negation of that which is false.

The global capitalism of today seems to be so successful only because its costs are externalized and thus partially invisible. In the last two centuries, humans and nature were exploited in the worst possible ways. While during "Manchester" capitalism, the local proletariat was suffering in our same latitudes of the Global North, the former colonies still continue to pay an even higher toll until this day.

This pattern has continued, where others are forced to pick up the tab, even during the thirty "glorious" years after the Second World War, in which the welfare state model functioned in many Western countries. At that time, hopes for other, more just societies were twinkling around the world. The previously colonized, now-independent states of the South were struggling for a new and more just world economic order. In the Eastern bloc, dissident notions of a socialism with a human face were articulated—for example, in Hungary in 1956 and in Czechoslovakia in 1968. The decade encompassing the year 1968 stood for worldwide revolt, (cultural) revolutions, and a new left.

The 1973 oil crisis, along with the abandonment of the fixed exchange rates of the Bretton Woods system and the transition away from Fordist and Taylorist production methods, marked the beginning of a dramatic neoliberal turn, with Ronald Reagan and Margaret Thatcher leading the way, proclaiming together that "There is no such thing as society."

A densely entangled global economy had already existed for some time. But with the massive outsourcing of labor—initially within North America and Europe and then to the workbenches of China and the rest of South Asia—we ushered in an era of accelerated globalization of commodity flows and capital.

Numerous countries in Latin America and the other continents took on enormous debt. This "odious debt" has enabled dictatorial and corrupt elites to continue to keep their societies shackled. The structural adjustment programs imposed by the World Bank and IMF, the policies of privatization and commodification of communal goods and property, and the sell-off of raw materials that these organizations prescribed, did not lead to any improvements.

As described by economist Thomas Piketty and others, global inequality—with all its consequences—increased as the rich got richer from inheritance and estates, primarily from stock ownership and its corresponding profit dividends. The poor became poorer. Meanwhile, the social systems of the West were more or less whittled down, as the progressive tax systems were being restructured. Often, these developments were legally secured and legitimized. UN Special Rapporteur Philip Alston called this glaring inequality in the world the "antithesis of human rights."

None of the crises of the last 15 years have been solved in a sustainable manner and the manifold problems persist. The euro crisis is once again intensifying in the current moment, recalling a similar situation after the global economic crisis of 2008, when the banks were subsidized but the financial system was not sufficiently reformed, and systemic deficiencies were not rectified. Thus, economic and social problems—such as inequality and climate change—are now looming larger.

In particular, corporate power—the power of oligarchs, corporations and the financial sector—has not been adequately contained politically. Indeed, some tax loopholes were closed in the EU, and EU Commissioner Margrethe Vestager vigorously cracked down on Apple and other digital companies. Yet, in line with their own national interests, many EU governments continue to offer the best possible conditions to large corporations, including tax cuts and subsidies. These corporate profits are not appropriately taxed in the areas where they accrue, while at the same time, a financial transaction tax and the stronger taxation of digital corporations have also been prevented.

Thus, even in the midst of the current crisis, there is still a danger that especially the big players will capture the enormous national and EU subsidies. Last, but not least, the revolving-door effect, the constant movement of personnel from politics to business and vice versa, generates incestuous relationships, fostering conflicts of interest, corruption and nepotism. Along these lines, the Bertelsmann Stiftung claimed in its 2020 Transformation Index Report: "Governments and their associated business elites use pre-existing privileges to consolidate their power and enrich themselves." This "clientelist form of power" is increasingly having a strong influence on democratically elected governments as well.

What is produced is not what is socially needed—such as medicine and personal protective equipment. It is not the social value of an activity that determines one's wages. Otherwise, nurses, caregivers, domestic helpers, cashiers and warehouse workers at Amazon would be paid much more. Only in some wealthy countries like Germany are the dispossessed at least to some extent protected, whereas elsewhere in the world, they are defenseless in the face of ongoing exposure to the pandemic and its impacts.

A particular expression of this increasing global economic inequality is growing hunger. According to the UN report "The State of Food Security and Nutrition in the World," 690 million people—or nine percent of the world's population—were already suffering from hunger in 2019, along with many more from malnutrition. According to more recent estimates, if the trend continues, the number is expected to rise to 840 million people by 2030 due to the economic consequences of the lockdowns.

The way the current situation is being handled, especially in countries ruled by authoritarian regimes, makes a mockery of the suffering and problems of many people. The countries of the pompous presidents Trump, Putin, Bolsonaro, Johnson, and Modi have the most infections and the most deaths in connection with COVID-19 worldwide. These leaders have unmasked themselves as incompetent, negligent criminals.

It never ceases to be shocking how the simplistic recipes of these populists—such as the authoritarian myths of renationalization and border closures—still seem to work.

The trend toward "autocratic entrenchment," according to the Bertelsmann Stiftung, is on the rise. Depending on the circumstances, autocratic repression is legitimized by anti-terrorism legislation, external enemies, or other alleged dangers. This process of policing and militarization of social conflicts is particularly evident in Eastern Europe and Russia—but also in Asia and parts of Latin America. The state of emergency is used by rulers like Modi in India or Orbán in Hungary to further expand their power. But this is not really so surprising. Every previous political opportunity was missed to curtail these manipulators by imposing sanctions within the EU or on trade and economic policy negotiations.

Instead of strengthening health systems worldwide and seriously addressing political solutions—such as creating a multilateral approach to complex global problems like the pandemic or the climate crisis—technological solutions (first and foremost surveillance) are being discussed. This can mean Orwellian, Chinese state capitalism with its ever-increasing surveillance of the entire population or the milder versions in Western Europe and North America. The current pandemic situation is also being exploited by European states like France to test out monitoring instruments such as drones or smartphone location tracking on a mass scale or—in the case of Spain—deploying the army on the streets. Critics of these measures are often accused of siding with right-wing Covid deniers.

The consequence of these tendencies is the shrinking space for civil society on a global scale. According to a 2019 report by CIVICUS (the World Alliance for Citizen Participation), governments in three-quarters of 196 countries took action against human rights defenders, NGOs, or political activists. In China, East Asia, the Arabian Peninsula, the Middle East, Russia, Turkey, and Hungary, the hope for civil society as a potential vehicle for political change is coming under pressure. But as the murders of Daphne Caruana Galizia in Malta and Ján Kuciak in Slovakia prove, the lives of journalists are no longer safe even in the European Union, when investigating the gray area between corruption, money laundering, and politics. A mix of administrative and punitive measures is used to harass numerous individuals and groups across Europe who show solidarity with refugees or rescue them from peril at sea.

In many states, police and other armed uniformed personnel are increasingly used for tasks beyond crime fighting. Cracking down on petty crime and deviant everyday behavior has been prioritized over adequately punishing the much more socially damaging crimes of million-dollar fraud and environmental destruction. The resistance undertaken by affected groups is often met with armed response. Stun guns, tear gas, and rubber bullets cause substantial injuries, as seen most recently in the democratic protests in France and Chile, where hundreds of people suffered eye injuries. The increasingly violent police apparatuses are becoming more powerful, while also enjoying more freedom from legal accountability and immunizing themselves against criticism.

But in Germany and Europe as well, the current crisis is accelerating such disastrous developments as the intensification of class antagonisms within school and university education. Digitalization without appropriate social controls leads not only to more surveillance, but also to changes in culture and communication. Last, but not least, the existence of public and alternative spaces are threatened by gentrification in our cities. These are not just cultural institutions in the strict sense, but spaces where people gather and meet, talk and engage with another, where free spaces, ideas, and concepts for action can emerge beyond the yoke of consumerism.

And although it is becoming increasingly clear that all these complex problems cannot be solved within a national framework alone, "the cosmopolitan consciousness" (Ulrich Beck) of societies is lagging behind. It is true, as Jürgen Habermas states, that there is no "linear connection between the Gini coefficient of an economy and the emergence of identitarian, nationalist and racist movements." The "institutional construction and expansion of democratically controlled transnational regimes" could create a pathway leading out of "the impasse of neoliberal governance..." Multilateralism is in crisis, partly because the existing supra- and transnational institutions—such as the UN or the EU—are not sufficiently democratically controlled and do not have the necessary power to adequately address the problems identified in their reports.

The perennial "us vs. them dichotomy" is leading to the disastrous re-nationalization of Europe and the rise of populist, right-wing movements and parties. The case of Hungary clearly illustrates the dangers: once in government, the nationalists restrict the free spaces for culture and civil society and put the stability of the law—especially the rights of minorities—into question, and thus expose entire demographic groups, such as the Roma, Sinti, and refugees, to state and societal violence.

Globally, according to WHO, the already overwhelming scale of (domestic) violence against women and children has increased in recent months due to the cramped conditions during the lockdown.

According to the International Lesbian, Gay, Bisexual, Trans and Intersex Association (ILGA), seventy-two countries worldwide have anti-gay laws in place, amounting to thirty-seven percent of all countries. Thirteen countries in Africa and Asia—including Iran, Saudi Arabia and parts of Nigeria—even administer the death penalty for homosexuality.

The danger of war, even nuclear war, as well as the number of active conflicts are increasing because of the internationalization of religious agitation. A new wave of nuclear armament is expected in the wake of the cancellation of the US-Russian INF agreement on nuclear arms control. In its 2020 yearbook, the Stockholm International Peace Research Institute (SIPRI) counted nineteen armed conflicts worldwide, of which those in Afghanistan, Syria,

Yemen, Mexico, and Nigeria were the most severe. A total of 70.8 million people are forcibly displaced, of which 25.9 million are refugees. According to UN Refugee Commissioner Filippo Grandi, this is also "no longer a short-term or passing phenomenon."

The drastic consequences of climate change are vividly described in the World Climate Report, such as the retreat of Arctic sea ice, the resulting rise of the oceans, the disappearance of virgin forests, and the extinction of species. Extreme weather events are becoming more frequent. Particularly alarming are the looming tipping points within ecosystems like the Amazon region or Siberia, for example. When reached, these ecosystems can no longer be saved, which will have far-reaching consequences for the entire planet.

Instead of addressing these new complex threats as a global community and looking after the well-being of the Earth and its inhabitants, the major players and regional powers and their associated economic entities are staking out their spheres of influence to develop new profit opportunities in the Arctic, for example.

This may appear to be an oversimplified dystopian scenario, but it isn't hard to imagine more catastrophic details further enriching this complex picture.

"But where there is danger, salvation grows as well," says German poet Friedrich Hölderlin. Many of the problems described here are being protested locally and globally; non-governmental organizations and the media are reporting on these grievances, and international coalitions are forming to fight them. This will be addressed in the next chapter.

3

Contested Fields—Resistance is Everywhere: On Utopias and Heterotopias

To counteract the gloominess of the previous chapter, I want to highlight how all over the world, people and organizations are fighting for a just and free society using intellectual critique and activist approaches.

In the spirit of Bloch, these endeavors—as a determinate negation of the false—can already be identified as an initial step into the utopian. For Bloch, "informed discontent" belongs to hope "because they both arise out of the No to deprivation." The well-founded critique, for example, of globalized and digitalized capitalism and the imperial way of life—of racism and misguided environmental policies—constitutes the basis for action of many committed people and groups. Authors such as Harald Welzer (*Everything could be different: A social utopia for free people*), Maja Göpel (*Rethinking Our World: An Invitation to Rescue Our Future*), Naomi Klein (*Green New Deal*), and the Latin American post-growth theorists Arturo Escobar and Maristela Svampa have recently argued in a more optimistic, less alarmist tone for major social changes.

The community of nongovernmental organizations and social movements is diverse and fragmented, even if one limits the focus only to those actively advocating for human rights in the broadest sense. There are also many particular single-issue movements. However, apart from their important temporary mobilization of people into the squares and the streets, it is unclear whether they are able and willing to work politically in the long term to realize the changes they demand. Nevertheless, they have committed themselves to actual struggles, and this already provides a context to manifest utopian elements. In recent decades alone, a myriad array of social movements has stitched itself together. The individual actors, although lacking a uniform program, have networked themselves both continentally and transnationally. They have accepted the complexity of each other's fields as a challenge, and this combined expertise produces new horizons for transformation.

The anti-globalization movement No Logo ("Another world is possible") gathered in the late 1990s and early 2000s at summits and anti-summits in Seattle, Porto Alegre, and Davos. Other important protagonists in this struggle were the primarily Latin American peasant movement La Via Campesina (The Peasant Way) with 200 million organized small farmers and the Landless Workers Movement, or Movimento dos Trabalhadores Rurais Sem Terra (MST) in Brazil, who are fighting for land reforms. These movements may not have stopped the fatal march of globalized capitalism. Nevertheless, they offered important networking and, above all, discursive potential, for example, from Joseph Stiglitz, Naomi Klein, Jean Ziegler, and Noam Chomsky.

In this regard, Occupy Wall Street, the 2011–2012 plaza occupations in Athens and Madrid, as well as mobilizations against free trade agreements, share a lineage with the critical analyses of globalization that surfaced at the turn of the millennium. But also, the more specialized, issue-based movements that advocate for solidarity with individual countries or for debt relief for states in the Global South, for fiscal justice and the abolition of tax havens, and for Attac's efforts to push through a financial transaction tax, have drawn upon these earlier struggles.

History has ups and downs; the end is not foreseeable. What is foreseeable is that movements are followed by counter-movements, setbacks are followed by progress. What we observe is contingent, neither foreordained nor impossible. As Niklas Luhmann puts it—it could thus be quite different.

This is perhaps most clearly felt in Latin America. The Mexican Zapatistas built an alternative autonomous region—a more-or-less liberated territory in Chiapas in southern Mexico—in which they tried out collective forms of ownership, models of self-management, and grassroots democracy. They also successfully networked with other indigenous and leftist groups within their own state and inspired rural and urban organizations worldwide with their lived practice, while simultaneously maintaining their utopian vision. In Bolivia, large progressive organizations emerged from the indigenous mobilizations of the 1990s and 2000s, such as the right-to-water campaign and the land struggles, some of which were able to assume governmental power. This movement—dubbed the pink tide or new progressivism—is rightly criticized by leftist, indigenous, and grassroots movements for its perpetuation of the neoliberal economic model and commodity extractivism—postcolonial continuities which have come at the price of the exploitation of nature, along with many murders of human rights defenders, women, and environmental activists. But with the constitutions forged by the new generations in Bolivia and Ecuador, they made legal history, even without the actual implementation of the rights granted on paper. The Lula government's fight against poverty is also part of this movement. It is said that more than 40 million poor people were wrested from their seemingly unchangeable fates, which can confidently be called historic. The backlash, however, did not take long to materialize. The seizure of power by right-wing governments in Paraguay, Bolivia, Honduras, Brazil—some of which used putschist methods—illustrates this. In the meantime, however, there have also been reversals, for example, in Argentina, where the neoliberal president Mauricio Macri was only able to hold on for four years. In any case, the region refuses to settle down. This is meant positively, as shown, for example, by the mass mobilization against the neoliberal economic and political system in 2019, by the successful referendum for a new constitution in Chile, and by the women's movement in Argentina and other Latin American countries.

Just looking at the activities of the last ten years is an exciting, surprising, and satisfying undertaking. India is not discussed much, but the number of people there working for democratic conditions is just as incredible as the uprisings in Hong Kong, Lebanon, or Sudan that have flared up out of nowhere.

In contrast, Europe is placid. Squatters and mobilizations against EU austerity programs led to party formations in Spain and Greece about ten years ago. However, with the defeat of Syriza and the continuing strength of right-wing populist movements, a political chill has returned.

The yellow vests protests in France are more difficult to categorize: they are undogmatic, they occupy public spaces (both symbolic and real), and they demonstrate once again that nothing happens without assembling in the streets. The movement invokes the principles of equality and fraternity of the French Revolution. The yellow vests refuse to act as a party, tending instead toward "degagism," which demands that all politicians immediately "get lost," and would rather accept this (power) vacuum than "business as usual." This causes problems for both the elites and the intellectuals close to them. However, the anti-Semitic and macho slogans and tendencies on the fringes of the movement cannot be overlooked either.

With the rise of right-wing populist and extreme right-wing organizations in Europe who have seated their beliefs in left-wing theorists such as Antonio Gramsci, many categories that were previously viewed unreservedly as positive by leftists—such as social movements, hegemony, and the blanket criticism of elites—have instead led to new ambivalence. Injustices and problems, real and perceived alike, are attributed to "the other," and verbal and viral agitation is often followed by pogrom-like riots and attacks. Because they disregard the dignity, life, and physical integrity of so many, these movements will not be discussed below. In practical, human rights-oriented politics these negative points of view must be fought. Resistance is forged in wretched circumstances.

After September 11, 2001, and the subsequent dominance of the terrorism paradigm and "surveillance capitalism," a worldwide movement grew out of smaller, specialized groups of hackers, such as the Chaos Computer Club and Wikileaks, alongside the civil rights organizations that had been active for some time. Initially, this movement only had moderate success in stopping mass surveillance, as its opponents at the time seemed to be overpowering. However, following the revelations of Edward Snowden in 2013, the movement did bring previously little-known facts to light around the world, thus bringing the problem to the attention of many new people.

The incitement and fury against migrants and racism has infected sectors of the population and politics in almost all European countries. It is often overlooked that the summer of migration in 2015 was also an act of resistance by the refugees themselves: predominantly Syrian migrants joined forces, crossed borders together, and thus created an undeniable new reality. The alliances of refugees from very different geographical and class constellations at the external borders were striking. Equally remarkable were the "welcome" movements, in Germany, for example, and the countless local efforts to help those who took refuge here to live in dignity or, in the case of the sea rescue initiatives, to migrate to Europe.

Up until now, little has been said about trade unions and the classical labor movement. In recent times, they have envisioned themselves as only representing the interests of those employees who make up their own ranks, and not as representing all the wretched of this earth who live in their own national territories and beyond, as was once the claim of the International. Not least for this reason, participation in trade unions—and thus their importance—has declined in the highly developed economies. However, trade union and strike movements are now forming at companies such as Ryanair and Amazon—although within these entities, with their precarious and individualized working conditions, this trade union activity is sometimes even prohibited.

It also exciting that cross-border initiatives for a minimum basic income, such as the Basic Income Earth Network, have begun to gain momentum during the Covid crisis. The cooperative movements and those advocating for the expansion of "commons" in their various guises are also winning supporters.

A separate chapter could also be devoted to all the movements in cities that oppose gentrification and the commodification of housing and home ownership, movements fighting for solidarity-based, car-free cities and cities that offer a livable environment for all.

One could go on to mention the important modes of self-organization of LGBTQIA+ people, the advocacy for transgender rights, and the attendant recent legal and political successes for these groups without hiding the fact that in large parts of the world, it is still a danger to one's life and freedom to openly live out one's sexuality.

Three movements are of particular importance for the assertion of human rights: the women's movement, the environmental movement, and Black Lives Matter (BLM).

The women's movement can look back on a long intellectual, as well as organizational, tradition, both in Germany and worldwide. The global movement, which is currently so strong in mobilization, builds upon this historical bedrock.

In the nineteenth century, it was predominantly the demands for general equality—specifically the right to education and for women's suffrage—that led to the formation of the Allgemeiner Deutscher Frauenverein (ADF) and many other organizations. The women's movement created transnational organizations, including the International Women's Suffrage Alliance (IWSA) (founded in Berlin in 1904 and later renamed the International Women's Alliance (IWA)) and the Women's International League for Peace and Freedom (WILPF) (founded in The Hague in 1915 during World War I). These organizations advocated internationally for women's suffrage and for articulated women's rights, drafting a program that included both political and social women's rights. This tradition of the women's movement extends into the 1990s with the major World Conferences on Women and Human Rights and their slogan "Women's Rights are Human Rights."

The international campaign against sexual harassment and violence triggered in 2017 by the hashtag #MeToo continues to have a major impact in the cultural sector as well. Though much of the original discussion essentially took place on social, as well as traditional, media platforms, the initiatives of the Argentine and Latin American women's movement marked a new phase of mobilization in the public space. Since 2016, Argentine women organized hundreds of thousands of women under the slogan #NiUnaMenos (Not One Less), acting initially against sexual violence, rape, and femicide, and for the right to abortion. This impetus was also taken up and carried further elsewhere.

As claimed in the call "Women of America: We are going to strike," co-authored by Angela Davis in the wake of the huge Women's March against Donald Trump in January 2017, violence against women cannot be separated from

> the violence of the market, of debt, of capitalist property relations, and of the state; the violence of discriminatory policies against lesbian, trans and queer women; the violence of state criminalization of migratory movements; the violence of mass incarceration; and the institutional violence against women's bodies through abortion bans and lack of access to free healthcare and free abortion.

These struggles do not only manifest themselves within demonstrations, but also in organized mass strikes from 2017 onwards. In 2018 alone, six million people took to the streets in Latin America (Argentina, Chile, Peru) and Spain. The mass strike is conceived as a process rather than an event, and unlike traditional union strikes, it aims to bring together not only workers from the production sector, but also those from the informal economies of labor.

This new feminist wave is distinguished by the fact that it represents an International in the making: local movements are networking on a continental and transnational level to jointly formulate demands and develop forms of action. In addition, it has transformative potential because it raises political-economic demands that go beyond calling for an end to structural violence. This does not only concern equal pay for equal work—demanded by the classical bourgeois women's movement—or quotas within universities and the management sector, but also the far-reaching discrimination against and devaluation of female work on all levels of society, as well as in all kinds of domestic, care, and reproductive work ("Care Revolution"), including precarious workers and migrants. In the United States, two million women took to the streets on 8 March 2017, following a call by the platform #feminism4the99%, which, as the name suggests, explicitly links itself to Occupy Wall Street and also has an anticapitalist thrust.

The Fridays for Future movement, along with many other groups such as Weed and Extinction Rebellion, also managed to propel an already strong global environmental movement to a new level during 2019. Some of the precursors to today's movements date back to the last century. The environmental movement took off in the 1970s, fueled by alarming studies, such as those by the Club of Rome (*The Limits to Growth*, 1972), leading repeatedly to new forms of protest, as seen in the anti-nuclear movement, and institutionalizing itself by the founding of the Green Party in Germany and elsewhere. Large and effective organizations such as Greenpeace and Robin Wood continuously combined education and criticism with spectacular actions and thus achieved considerable political success.

Fierce conflicts took place in many countries of the South, as evidenced by the murders of the environmentalist Chico Mendes in Brazil in 1988, the writer Ken Saro-Wiwa in 1995 (who campaigned in Nigeria against the pollution of the Niger Delta by the Shell oil company), and the lawyer and environmental activist Digna Ochoa in Mexico in 2001.

Through the mobilization of young people in school strikes, the demonstrations of the last two years, and the broaching of questions of intergenerational justice, the issue has gained new traction in a synchronized fashion all over the world—even if the prominence of the environmental movement is threatened by suppression in pandemic times. It is thanks to the movements—not only in Europe but also in the Global South—that climate justice and global justice are being named and addressed as outgrowths of the same systemic problem. The connections between climate catastrophe and colonial land expropriation have increasingly been rendered visible, and fossil fuel companies are being held responsible for causing a significant share of harmful emissions. In addition, the movements counter the myths of the economy of perpetual growth and its benefits for all. That's why they have transformative potential that will last beyond 2019.

Black Lives Matter, in turn, builds on centuries of resistance to slavery, from the "riders" to the "freedom riders" of the civil rights movement, Martin Luther King, the Black Panthers, and countless historical layers of local—as well as national—intellectual and artistic revolt.

The "Black Revolution was much more than a struggle for the rights of Negroes," according to Martin Luther King in 1969. It forced "America to face all its interrelated flaws: racism, poverty, militarism, materialism." The evils of this society, he said, are "rooted deeply in the structure of society." Therefore, "radical reconstruction of society itself is the real issue to be faced."

Mass unemployment and the disproportionate death toll of Black people during the COVID-19 crisis fueled the protest. The momentum with which a wide variety of groups joined together and demonstrated *en masse* in every major city in the United States may have surprised many. However, without the organizing work of recent years and the critique of historical injustice, it would hardly have been conceivable.

What initially appeared as massive solidarity rallies across much of Europe quickly grew to challenge structurally racist ideologies and practices in France, Britain, and Germany. The wave also captured the historical injustice of colonialism in Europe, the consequences of which can still be seen and felt today in the former colonies, as well as in the former colonial powers—for example, in Belgium and Great Britain, but also in Germany.

What looked to a broader public like a spontaneous uprising in the US in response to the assassination of

George Floyd in fact took place thanks to a tightly woven network of organizational efforts and intellectual engagement with historical racism, along with its current manifestations. Although past efforts to obtain reparations for slavery did not meet with immediate success, Ta-Nehisi Coates's 2014 article "The Case for Reparations" in *The Atlantic* magazine inspired a great deal of academic, legal, and political activity. BLM's success and intellectual content rest on these developments, as well as on the analyses of Keeanga-Yamahtta Taylor and others who have traced the causes and forms of poverty among Black people, and the economic inequality between Black and white people in all its facets over the past 80 years.

The question does arise, however, as to why human rights (at least those explicitly expressed as such) only play a rather subordinate role in the context of the three aforementioned movements, and why, for example, the trade unions, Black movements, and the women's movement do not make more frequent use of the human rights paradigm.

In fact, during their history, all these movements have invoked human rights and understood themselves (at least also) as human rights organizations. Already in the late nineteenth and early twentieth century, for example, forms of internationalized group solidarity emerged, most clearly in the women's movement. The two best-known representatives of the US civil rights movement also frequently made reference to human rights. Malcolm X, representing 22 million African Americans at a meeting of the Organization of African States (OAS) in 1964, emphasized that at its core, the problem was neither "a Black problem, nor an American problem," but a problem of the world and for humanity, and "not a problem of civil rights," but "a problem of human rights."

Other African American organizations submitted numerous petitions to the United Nations in the postwar decades. Even Martin Luther King, during his final months, repeatedly spoke of a human rights revolution in order to situate the political struggle of African Americans in the context of a worldwide freedom movement of peoples.

And for the labor movement as well, it has always been true that "workers' rights are human rights." Thus, the core labor standards of the International Labor Organization (ILO), including prohibitions on forced labor and child labor, are categorized as universal human rights.

Nowadays, a more heterogenous picture is emerging. In places where dictatorships ruled just a short time ago, large sections of civil society are working to come to terms with this troubled past, particularly in Latin America. Human rights has also been explicitly invoked in current struggles for women's or indigenous rights, as well as in confrontations with mining and other transnational corporations. These movements take advantage of various tried-and-true tactics, such as mass demonstrations, occupations, but also in opinion tribunals. Artistic displays and lawsuits in court often go hand in hand. Due to the specific legal situation in the US, Black Lives Matter activists are more likely to sue for constitutional rights—as human rights are less popular as a topos.

Traditional human rights organizations are also not likely to be present in efforts to address European colonialism.

Human rights appear even less explicitly in the discourse of North American and European environmental and climate activists—even though an appeal to human rights would make sense in many respects. Many problematic situations can also be understood in terms of human rights, for example, such as the rights to life, bodily integrity, and the collective rights of animals and nature. Human rights categories can also be used to grasp various non-European circumstances, such as rights to water, food, and decent housing, as well as basic social security.

With these contexts in mind, the Eurocentric view can be broadened, and the renewed turn to patriarchal savior fantasies within conservative environmental organizations can be avoided. Moreover, while procedures and forums, such as UN complaint mechanisms or international courts, do not offer solutions to complex global problems, they can provide another platform to address these concerns. The rights to property and the unimpeded acquisition of profits claimed by corporations and banks would be more strongly countered in these various forums, including arbitration tribunals.

I will briefly take up these issues again in the concluding chapter. But first, I would now like to talk about the modern human rights movement and its best-known organization, Amnesty International, which explicitly sees the defense of human rights as its mandate.

4

The Human Rights Movement
as (Part Of) the Solution?

Instrumentalization and skepticism

Today, many activists and leftists in the Global North and South are skeptical about the concept of human rights. One reason for this may be that human rights have often only existed on paper. Unsurprisingly, these mere rights did not have the power to change the world. The fact that they nevertheless did bring about positive changes is overlooked, which will be discussed in the final chapter.

Another reason is the instrumentalization of human rights by powerful protagonists and the ease with which they appropriated the human rights discourse. In *Morals of the Market: Human Rights and the Rise of Neoliberalism*, Australian lawyer Jessica Whyte traces the links between neoliberal theory and human rights back to the 1940s, when the new world order was being negotiated. For neoliberals such as the Mont Pelerin Society, a functioning market requires the rule of law and a moral foundation—and thus requires human rights. But, once again, this certainly does not grant them the status of being the sole proprietors of the post-war human rights project, to which many other actors have laid claim. But it does explain a reading of human rights—and the attempts at their appropriation—that has been virulent ever since.

After the disasters of the Vietnam War and the Watergate scandal, the United States—notably under President Jimmy Carter—turned to human rights as a new source of "American values." This occurred at a time when almost the entire Latin American continent, including Central America, was being harassed by militaries trained by the US.

In addition, there was the attempt to instrumentalize the discourse of human rights in the so-called Helsinki process, which refers to the 1975 Helsinki Final Act of the OSCE states under the leadership of the United States. This process was less concerned with the realization of universal human rights than with making the other side look bad. One of the founders of Human Rights Watch, Aryeh Neier, wrote of the establishment of Helsinki Watch (later Human Rights Watch—today one of the most influential human rights organizations) that it had exploited the power of the United States in the world to advance its own agenda. The idea behind this was that there was a center, namely, New York and the United States, and a periphery, the 1970s Eastern Bloc and the Third World. The New Left, the anti-imperialist left, half of Latin America, and especially postcolonial critics around the world were suspicious of this concept.

Moreover, from the 1990s onward, the US and NATO invoked the concept of humanitarian intervention in their attacks on Yugoslavia, Iraq, and Libya, which in its patterns of justification resembled the so-called civilizing missions that were used to legitimize colonialism and imperialism.

Thus, for many contemporaries, human rights no longer stood for revolutionary ideals, but for bigoted policies and military strikes by the West.

The problem is not so much that this dimension of recent human rights history exists. After all, other progressive categories such as democracy and freedom have always been claimed by a wide variety of political thinkers. But this perspective still heavily shapes the concept of human rights today for many people who could otherwise potentially be mobilized for human rights work.

The most successful: Amnesty International

But what do the human rights politics of human rights organizations look like in the broader sense?

Already in the 19th century, organizations existed that had human rights on their agenda, such as primarily religious (especially Jewish) groups and women's and pacifist organizations. But large international associations specializing in human rights, such as those we have today, did not exist before the founding of Amnesty International (AI) in 1961. AI initially recruited its members from among the ranks of intellectuals and professionals in order to help political prisoners. The various names of the organization—first Appeal for Amnesty and then Amnesty International—stood for both its substantive program, as well as its chosen method. The primary method at the time was organized letter-writing campaigns to ask governments to grant amnesty—or mercy—to prisoners.

As the co-founder of the German chapter, Gerd Ruge, explains, the very fact that the organization advocated equally for Western and Eastern prisoners of conscience already represented a form of "détente politics" and the "concrete negation of the Cold War logic" that had polarized West German society and half the world at the time.

Accordingly, AI chose a path that did not question power or systems of domination in general. The focus was limited to prisoners of conscience who used non-violent means to stand up for their political and otherwise divergent views. This excluded those who used violent means to rebel against unjust forms of rule such as colonial systems. Because of this broad concept of impartiality—and despite stark criticism—AI did not oppose apartheid in South Africa as a system.

On this subject, former AI Secretary General Thomas Hammarberg claimed in 1986 in the news magazine *Der Spiegel*: "We do not touch on the roots of oppression. We are neither for nor against any particular ideology or policy, do not take sides with Marxism, liberalism, or whatever else. We take on the symptoms of oppression alone— torture, political imprisonment, denial of basic rights."

This is "Amnesty's strength," which is why "people of the most diverse worldviews" can work with them. This is not only the DNA of the world's most important human rights organization in recent history, but also the DNA of a broad segment of the Western human rights movement, along with its collective notion of what human rights work should look like.

In the course of the 1970s, AI advanced groundbreaking positions on such overarching issues as the abolition of torture, the fight against the death penalty, extrajudicial executions, and enforced disappearances. The campaign against torture, in particular, brought media attention to the organization—and with this attention came new members and growing revenues. The organization was able to expand and professionalize. It was no coincidence that Amnesty International won the Nobel Peace Prize in 1977, the same year President Jimmy Carter took office in the United States.

Historian Samuel Moyn describes the entrance of human rights onto the world political stage as the new lingua franca of political morality and the story of the last remaining utopia. In the previous decade, colonial liberation movements, the New Left, the student movement, and Eastern European dissidents sought to radically change their societies and the world. After the failure of these grand political designs, more and more people turned toward an incrementalist politics defined by taking gradual steps.

Amnesty International met all the criteria for this, as historian Jan Eckel points out in his comprehensive study *The Ambivalence of Good.* The organization presented itself as ideologically and politically non-partisan, an approach still attractive to many in the human rights scene, especially lawyers, regardless of the changes that have since taken place in AI's organization and its concept. For the many younger and older well-educated, middle-class people from North America and Western Europe, AI provided an outlet for feelings of helplessness in the face of structures of power and indignation about injustices they had not experienced themselves, as well as for transforming any identification with the suffering of others into activism.

The price for this was a form of "reducing the complexity of politics" (Eckel). One would individualize and concretize an injustice and, yet, also "decontextualize" it at the same time. In order to maintain the claim to political neutrality, one worked primarily with descriptions and later with photos of those suffering individual fates. The suffering of others was meant to bring forth suggestions that would benefit a particular campaign, the Amnesty International organization, and the project of human rights as a whole.

However, this also created "a picture of violence that was as ubiquitous as it was anonymous, taking on a life of its own and ultimately even appearing inexplicable." (Eckel). Structural and systemic causes were bracketed or ignored. The logic of victimhood, which emphasized the suffering of those innocently tortured, was used instead of examining the systemic and structural causes of human rights violations. This culture—a first-person politics of victimhood—refused to engage in theoretical discussions, let alone political programs, which also alienated AI from the organized political left. It should be added that the recent history of the organized political left in Europe and the US has been marred by grandiose political errors and a lack of resounding successes.

Nobody had anything against Amnesty International; everybody wished them maximum success in their cause. But the organization aimed to moralize the substance of politics, the political *par excellence*, and not to fundamentally question or overturn the conditions that led to human rights violations. This approach is simultaneously the reason behind the organization's success story, as well as for the dilemma it still suffers from today.

The increased income, the growth in membership, and the great power of the organization— especially after the Nobel Peace Prize in 1977—led to the establishment of a powerful and professional apparatus in London.

Amnesty International's human rights reports, such as those on torture or on the situation in individual countries, stand for the organization like perhaps no other medium. In contrast to activist or small regional organizations, these reports still claim to research, compile, and evaluate the facts with the greatest possible accuracy. This sometimes takes more time than would be the most advantageous for the urgency of the matter. However, to ensure that the facts speak for themselves so that a report can carry the Amnesty International seal of credibility, there is hardly any alternative. The goal is to generate political pressure on the respective governments in the countries where AI's base is strongest and to chastise the governments under criticism in the eyes of the world public.

Because the organization successfully promotes its reports with great journalistic effort, effective publicity is practically guaranteed. Journalists and various political actors often make use of their work. The political impact of these reports, however, is debatable, though certainly not on the basis of simple rubrics. The publication of an abuse—even the creation of a public outcry—does not necessarily lead to the cessation of the human rights violations under criticism, let alone to the fight against their causes. On the other hand, reports and other actions by Amnesty have mobilizing effects within the membership of the organization and their countries of origin, as well as in the societies affected. At the very least, the organization almost always manages to educate, to generate public outcry, and to raise awareness about certain issues with its resources. That is no small feat.

Over the years, AI developed a differentiated approach to advocacy work within various political apparatuses, parliaments, and their respective publics. This entails advocating for human rights in political discourse and vis-à-vis political institutions in order to educate and influence political will. This still occurs predominantly in Western countries, where Amnesty International's sub-organizations with the largest membership are represented. With its campaigns against torture or enforced disappearance, and later for the judicial processing of human rights violations through international criminal law, the organization contributed to the establishment of new forms of international law at both national and international levels.

Amnesty International opens up

Since the days of the Cold War, the political climate has changed considerably. The principle of non-interference in internal affairs, which dominated international relations at the time, has given way to a new awareness of the need to take sides on human rights issues.

AI opened its doors to new issues following criticism from the Global South and discussions in the North, including economic and social rights after 2001. One example of this is the book on poverty published in 2009 by the then-General Secretary Irene Khan, in which she characterizes poverty as a violation of human rights.

The same can be said of Human Rights Watch: in addition to the classic cases of Belarus and Hong Kong, there are reports from 2020 on structural racism in the United States and corruption in Lebanon. Topics such as poverty, inequality, minimum basic income, and climate justice are also discussed.

Topics which cut across multiple fields, such as inequality and discrimination, are also emerging within Amnesty International's ongoing strategy debates, alongside the more traditional issues, such as freedom of expression and threats to civil society. The organization opened itself to new content and has further differentiated its efforts. The participatory element of the organization—both its strength and simultaneously the source of its substantial credibility—was further expanded, with membership in the Global South growing from two to 40 percent of the total organization within two decades. From then on, it was no longer the size of the individual sections that determined influence but, rather, the principle of "one section, one vote."

All these developments are the subject of heated, democratic debate within the organization. However, with the current expansion of the mandate and the general widening of the scope of issues addressed, a dilemma arose: the core elements of Amnesty's brand—visible and well known everywhere—have increasingly dissolved.

When he took office in 2018, former General Secretary Kumi Naidoo had already claimed that "the human rights movement needs to be bigger, bolder and more inclusive…" The world's complex problems could only be tackled, he said, if people freed themselves from the idea "that human rights are about some forms of injustice that some people face, but not others." In keeping with these sentiments, Naidoo reminds us that "the patterns of oppression we're living through," from the climate crisis to inequality to sexual discrimination, are "interconnected."

However, chronologically speaking, public perception lags behind these realities. Naidoo, a South African anti-apartheid campaigner, was able to articulate perspectives based on his personal experiences that were likely new not only to a portion of Amnesty International's membership, but also to much of the Western public. And yet: "said" does not automatically mean "done." The organizational structure built up over decades out of a strong apparatus and a large worldwide membership is not easy to control. Additionally, the underlying conditions for the work to be done in different countries could not be more different.

Postcolonial criticism of Western NGOs

Postcolonial legal theorists and activists have been criticizing Western human rights organizations for some time. For example, they criticize the long-standing focus on political and civil rights and the failure to engage in advocacy for collective economic and social rights. In addition, Western actors are faulted for dealing almost exclusively with rights violations in the Global South, as well as for doing so with an attitude of moral and civilizational supe-riority. In this fashion, they divide people into victims and perpetrators, claiming for themselves the role of savior, as the Kenyan-American professor Makau Mutua from the Buffalo School of Law (the influential co-founder of Third World Approaches to International Law, or TWAIL) so forcefully put it.

Indian writer Arundhati Roy also warns against the "NGO-ization" of politics because it threatens to turn resistance from below into a well-paid job. In India, she says, this has occurred in tandem with the retreat of the state, leading to the depoliticization of political struggle.

The postcolonial critique also applies to the compo-sition of Western organizations, whose members and leadership cadres were largely drawn from the educated middle classes in Western Europe and North America. The diversification and globalization of the organizations occurred late in the game. The social differences and the major biographical, linguistic, and cultural differences between the actors in the West and the rest of humanity are too quickly flattened in both public and internal dis-cussions. In particular, little is said about the privileged access to all kinds of resources that Western human rights activists often have. Frequently, this entails that those with money and other resources decide the agenda and priori-ties in a paternalistic way.

Mutua accuses them of using their "first world resources—money, political power, proximity to global hegemons" to reproduce "global power relations," which leads them to become "conservative, cautious, and supporters of the establishment." To overcome the imbalance between organizations based in the West and those based in the South, "genuine cross-border cooperation" between international and other NGOs will be necessary.

Tshepo Madlingozi, a professor and activist from South Africa, similarly characterizes what he calls "transitional justice entrepreneurs" as a well-traveled cadre of protagonists who describe the field, set the agenda, have the financial resources, advise governments and, in their view, invite and train relevant local NGOs and grassroots movements—all the while constantly claiming to speak about and for the victims, which actually serves to turn any victims into disempowered subjects.

In essence, this is also about money: non-governmental organizations are dependent on funding from private donors or foundations. They live from their reputations and thus also from successful self-promotion and marketing. For existential reasons alone, they are therefore concerned with generating attention and defending their reputations and market positions. Human rights work has now become monetized, at least in part. Thus, one is economically dependent on the success of one's own activities being communicated to the outside world in a perceptible way, as well as on the respective preferences of the sponsors and the structure of the funding cycles.

The capacity for public self-criticism is thus correspondingly low. Therefore, the narratives expressed in funding applications and public announcements, such as press releases, newspaper portraits, television reports, documentaries, and social media often determine both external and self-perception. In this context, narratives are often generated in which the white savior, usually from the North, is placed in the foreground of the reporting, while the local grassroots movements and participants are relegated to the background.

There is too little space for reflection and self-criticism—not even for voicing that which is self-evident or contradictory. Without funding from institutions that have acquired their money mostly through economic activities in the very same world market that is responsible for so many human rights abuses, most NGOs would not exist. Accordingly, many organizations in the metropole cities are staffed by professionals of all kinds from fundraising, communications, and digitalization campaigns who might work within various kinds of organizations during their careers.

Moreover, the legitimacy of non-governmental organizations is generally and quite rightly questioned—for example, in the case of associations that operate exclusively as lobbying entities, as well as from organizations that are covertly funded by governments. However, questions also remain about the financing models and the resulting dependence on sponsors.

The fact that organizations such as the US Ford Foundation and the Open Society Foundation stand for the free-market, democratic, liberal, and open model of society that is criticized elsewhere is—for these foundations—just as much a matter of pride as their philanthropic commitment. By the same token, one cannot reproach the human rights organizations for accepting funds from such organizations—as long as they do not come from actual arms companies. What is worthy of criticism, however, is that there is almost no political debate about these obvious facts. Instead, the sector behaves in a non-transparent and almost ignorant manner.

Outlook

Both Amnesty International and Human Rights Watch, as the two preeminent international human rights organizations, exemplify a particular political and organizational model with excellent access to all segments of the public. Due to their origins and methodological approaches, they may have limitations.

What seems problematic is that these two organizations—as well as other human rights-focused activities in The Hague, Geneva, New York and London—are the only representative entities of human rights work for much of the political and media public. While they may not explicitly demand this duopoly, nevertheless these few players dominate the international scene by virtue of their prominence and resourcing. Other actors, especially those not operating in the metropolitan areas, are often left out.

All over the world, new groups have formed that also work using legal means alongside and in the interest of affected communities. There are currently social movements that have broken down the division between political and civil rights versus economic and social rights. I will focus on this and on the use of transnational legal means in selected areas in the next section.

5

Legal Human Rights Work—
Struggles for Justice

It is an achievement that new norms for human rights protection and new judicial forums and UN procedures have been established since 1948. But how viable are these norms, and have they provided access to justice for those affected? Who are the actors who make use of these legal mechanisms?

That is what I would like to delve into in this chapter. It is somewhat lengthy, as it deals with my core activities and the work of my organization, the European Center for Constitutional and Human Rights (ECCHR). The latter's work may have influenced the selection of the constellation of cases described here, but I have tried to avoid engaging in any PR on my own behalf. Rather, I want to illustrate how different actors make use of the law and work concretely on the utopia of human rights through legal interventions.

Forums such as the European and Inter-American human rights systems have existed since 1959, but have remained dormant, as have many laws that could have been brought to bear on human rights matters. The reason things became increasingly dynamic over the years was because a network of human rights activists made better use of the laws and forums by taking legal action. Through the courts and their particular form of publicity, these activists, along with their communities and organizations, have opened up a new field of action for themselves since the 1990s.

Critical scholars have scrutinized the law in general and human rights in particular. The ambivalence and critiques surrounding the law and human rights standards are as practically relevant as they are theoretically relevant. Therefore, the legal actions concerning human rights taken in recent years will be examined more closely here.

On the one hand, legal frameworks protect against immediate, direct forms of the use of force. They can therefore have a protective function for refugees or prisoners, for example. On the other hand, law was and is part of the arsenal of systems of domination because it legally establishes unjust conditions, for example, in regard to property and the economic system.

A brief look at legal practice allows us to deconstruct the erroneous belief within human rights work that the adoption of laws and the ratification of conventions automatically translates their progressive content into reality without a confrontation with power.

The antislavery and labor movements of the past, in addition to the women's movement and the civil rights movement in the United States, always had legal means within their arsenal. In addition to mobilizations through demonstrations, mass strikes, reports, and political influence, they invoked human rights declarations or constitutions and used petitions and lawsuits to achieve their political goals. Unlike sectors of today's human rights scene and most lawyers, however, they never conceived of themselves as impartial or even politically neutral but, rather, integrated legal means into their political strategies. If anything, their struggles for workers', women's, and civil rights were successful because they combined mass mobilizations with political campaigns and legal actions.

As leftist jurist Jules Lobel points out in his book *Success without Victory*, political and legal successes in such processes have never been congruent. He cites examples from the fight against slavery and for women's suffrage, lawsuits against US military operations in Central America, and the closing of a steel mill in Youngstown, Ohio— each of which was a fight lost in court. Nevertheless, these lawsuits created a public platform for the respective causes that would not have existed without the lawsuits. For him, courts also represent forums of protest.

In the Anglo-American legal sphere—and after a considerable time lag, also in Europe—these strategic lawsuits are referred to as "strategic litigation." This term refers to lawsuits in the public interest that pursue political goals that extend beyond the immediate success of the lawsuits in and of themselves. The concept—which now includes a wide range of approaches—only refers to the activities of lawyers and their highly diverse clients. The litigation tactic of strategic litigation has also been used by business lawyers or right-wing, populist plaintiffs—for example, in the constitutional complaints in Germany against the European Central Bank.

Nor does the term encompass all legal actions. After all, some lawsuits were not planned long in advance and were not strategic. Rather, in certain cases, successful means were simply implemented at the right moment, opportunistically taking advantage of the right constellation of circumstances. Nevertheless, some such opportunistic legal actions led to "unimaginable" results, as in the criminal complaint against the Chilean ex-dictator Augusto Pinochet.

Some trials that culminated in defeat in judicial contexts still had a mobilizing effect for the political struggle of a respective group. In other cases, court proceedings that succeeded turned out to be a Pyrrhic victory, because the rulings were not politically implemented, or were implemented inadequately, and also tied up resources and attention. The relationship between legal steps and political and social mobilization, such as public relations work, can thus not be described in an abstract manner, but must be defined according to the specific nature of each situation.

In the post-war decades, few actors resorted to transnational legal remedies. Malcom X and other civil rights activists, for example, approached the UN with petitions against the discrimination of Black people on several occasions, but without any resounding success. It was simply not a common approach.

This was not only because of the fact that the 1948 "Universal Declaration of Human Rights" was not legally binding. States had it in their power to bind themselves according to their own constitutions and through international treaties. The number of covenants (and their content) on political and civil, as well as economic, social, and cultural rights—in addition to the conventions on, for example, international humanitarian law, the prohibition of torture, and the labor and social standards in the conventions of the International Labor Organization (ILO)—are numerous and imposing. Many of the atrocities and some forms of exploitation that still take place today are legally outlawed. But there often remains a lack of legal avenues and forums that enable affected people to claim their rights, or else people simply do not have access to justice in the first place. In the closed societies of China, Russia, or North Korea, for example, many of the basic requirements for the rule of law are missing.

The struggle for justice and human rights therefore entails that different actors act from their respective positions and that, in the best case, their activities may complement each other in the political struggle for more humane norms and to create fair and independent judicial systems. But in addition to the normative and institutional changes necessary, the law must also be made accessible to everyone in practice, which means that civil society actors must in turn intervene concretely at various levels, often in confrontation with powerful forces, while still mobilizing public opinion.

The fact that, even in the case of victorious judicial verdicts, practices which violate human rights have not been abolished at the international and transnational levels is due—in the case of international institutions—to the lack of a world state to enforce the law, to a fragmented system of global jurisdiction, and to the contradictions, for example, between international trade law and the corpus of human rights law.

Nevertheless, after all national legal channels were exhausted, and especially after the expansion of human rights protection systems from the 1970s onward in Europe and the Americas, affected parties and civil society actors initiated human rights lawsuits before the two human rights courts in Strasbourg and San José in Costa Rica, and later before UN tribunals and European courts according to the principle of universal jurisdiction. Here, we will focus more closely on the two fields in which transnational strategic lawsuits have been brought by civil society actors for several decades: international criminal law and business and human rights.

At first, there were only a few cases in which the international community addressed the most serious human rights violations after 1945.

International Crimes and International Criminal Law

Criminal law, especially international criminal law, has become one of the main fields of legal human rights work in the last twenty years. When the greatest possible harm to human rights has been done, and when genocide or crimes against humanity are committed, there is little space for utopian notions. Criminal law, of all things, enters the scene, which was perceived by leftist and progressive movements in various historical moments as an instrument of repression by states that are more or less authoritarian.

Ever since the Nuremberg trials of the chief Nazi war criminals, there have been debates about whether criminal law may be the right response to systemic injustice—that is, human rights violations committed and orchestrated by state apparatuses. This is because in criminal trials, the courts are limited to procedural truth and the determination of the guilt of individual perpetrators. This is criticized as the individualization of systemic injustice.

In the end, the positive lessons of the Nuremberg trials certainly prevailed: the fact that the victorious powers did not take revenge and carry out mass executions, but instead voluntarily handed over their "captive enemies to the judgment of the law," thus offering "...one of the most significant tributes that Power has ever paid to Reason," according to the US chief prosecutor Robert Jackson. For the first time, those who had committed genocide, war crimes, and wars of aggression had to answer to a court, even if they had committed such acts as members of a state apparatus that had authorized them to do so. But there was more at stake, as Robert Jackson so presciently put it in his closing argument: "And let me make clear that while this law is first applied against German aggressors, the law includes, and if it is to serve a useful purpose it must condemn aggression by, any other nations, including those which sit here now in judgment."

Expectations of justice in such criminal cases should not be too high. It would be good to keep in mind, as the writer Peter Weiss has claimed, that "the use of these means, which are hardly still suitable, is better than silence and bewilderment."

It does not speak well for the historical conscious-ness of today's contemporaries that these fundamental discussions are hardly pursued within the human rights debate. Today's trials before national and international criminal courts are often directed against rather subordi-nate perpetrators and rarely against the highest-ranking persons responsible. It is easier to furnish proof in cases against the immediate, primarily low-level perpetrators. If, on the other hand, a general or a defense minister is to be held criminally responsible for systematic torture or rape, the legal situation becomes more difficult, with mounting political pressure. As a result, such criminal trials are often piecemeal. This is rarely mentioned by those involved, as the relativization of such criminal acts would also diminish their importance.

In contrast, the agenda of the US prosecutors within the Nuremberg military tribunals in the follow-up pro-ceedings appears to be much more ambitious and more appropriate to crimes of this magnitude. On the basis of an analysis of the Nazi system of injustice, the responsibility of elite members of society within the National Socialist system was legally investigated with the help of important exiled intellectuals, leading to exemplary charges against individual industrialists, lawyers, physicians, as well as top leaders in the government, the military, in business, and in political parties. Due to the emergent constella-tions of power at the start of the Cold War, the follow-up proceedings were ultimately not carried through to the end, and the sentences handed down were not enforced because the old German elites were thought to be needed in the fight against communism, despite their involvement in Nazi crimes. Nonetheless, one would like to see more similarly bold, strategic policies of indictment today.

Following in the footsteps of US prosecutors Robert Jackson, Telford Taylor, and Benjamin Ferencz, the Hessian Attorney General Fritz Bauer at the time consistently sought to prosecute these Nazi injustices in West Germany in a hostile environment and despite a wide variety of restrictions. Without his work, the Auschwitz trials in Frankfurt am Main in the mid-1960s, which were so significant for the history of the Federal Republic, would probably not have been held.

These trials are also proof that the legal process itself is not always the decisive factor when compared to the social impact. In the trial, the Frankfurt Regional Court cemented a legal theory that was heavily criticized for a long time and only recently abandoned, according to which Nazi perpetrators could only be convicted when very specific criteria were met. Therefore, it was ultimately the reception of the trial events by journalists and artists such as Peter Weiss, Heiner Kipphardt, and Inge Deutschkron that contributed decisively to the social reckoning with Nazi crimes.

But no matter how commendably Jackson or Bauer each approached his respective complex of proceedings, these proceedings remained state-sponsored events, in which the survivors of the Holocaust, the relatives of the dead, and civil society forces played only a limited role, which Hannah Arendt in particular sharply criticized on the occasion of the Eichmann trial in Jerusalem.

The so-called opinion tribunals, which were called into being for the first time in 1967 by the mathematician and philosopher Bertrand Russell because of the war crimes committed by the United States in the Vietnam War, were clearly different. The chairman of the first public tribunal—the philosopher Jean-Paul Sartre—formulated one of the tribunal's goals as "to bring to life the law born early at Nuremberg and to apply ethical and legal rules to the law of the jungle."

The US prosecutors appointed to this task did not respond to the numerous war crimes committed by US troops in Vietnam. How could they? They would have needed to bring the US government to justice as the main perpetrator. Thus, legal challenges made little sense to the anti-war movement, so activists and intellectuals instead created the public opinion tribunals that still exist and are held to this day. These tribunals explicitly anchored themselves to legal principles and replicated the form and dramaturgy of court proceedings.

Probably the most effective and professional tribunal of this kind was convened in 2000 and 2001 regarding the forced prostitution by the Japanese military during World War II, which made a significant contribution to the further development of international law as a result.

The tribunals did not achieve the legitimacy of state institutions and proceedings. However, they were able to enlighten the public about unknown facts and—due to their special format—to highlight the failures of the state authorities who were actually responsible.

Beginning in the 1970s, the couple Serge and Beate Klarsfeld sought to bring the chief architects and executioners of the extermination of the Jews in Germany and France to justice. At the time, they were already carrying out public political actions, legal-journalistic research, and were active in court, which is why the two can be considered forerunners of today's human rights lawyers.

Their actions were creative and courageous, such as the public slap in the face of Nazi collaborator and German Chancellor Kurt-Georg Kiesinger and the attempted kidnapping of Kurt Lischka, one of the masterminds behind the extermination of Jews in France. Their undercover research led most famously to the trial in Lyon of the former head of the Gestapo, Klaus Barbie. Afterwards, high-ranking officials in the Nazi system, who had previously been excluded from prosecution, were finally brought to justice—albeit 25 to 30 years too late and inadequately. This made it clear not only to the French public, but above all to the German public, how great their failure had been in coming to terms with National Socialism, both legally and socially.

Lawyers who use legal means in the fight to address crimes against humanity have been around for decades. Civil society actors can be found among them, even if their contributions are hardly acknowledged by today's leaders.

Unimaginable: The Pinochet arrest in London in October 1998

While the Nuremberg trials were, according to their chief prosecutor, a "tribute that Power has paid to Reason," those affected by state violence soon fought for their own rights and trials. With the arrest of Chilean ex-dictator Augusto Pinochet in London on October 16, 1998, transnational human rights justice took off. The case had an enormous impact not only on those directly involved and on Chilean society, but on the human rights movement and international criminal law all over the world. Hardly anyone has put this unimaginable story into words as vividly as the exiled Chilean writer Ariel Dorfman did in his diary. "Have you heard of Pinochet? Oh my God. Not him again. Not Pinochet, not this early in the morning. Not ever. Pinochet? Pinochet? I was sick of Pinochet...He's been arrested in London...last night. Scotland Yard, acting on an order from a Spanish judge. I thought to myself, my mind automatically switching into the Spanish I bizarrely shared with General Pinochet: Esto tiene ques er un sueno. This must be a dream."

Dorfman describes what happened in the Belmarsh courtroom in London as something very dramatic: "For some people at least, the world had suddenly begun to turn in the opposite direction. For some people, life from now on would never be the same."

By this, Dorfman meant the arrest of his own country's despot, formerly considered untouchable, who had arrogated to himself the role of master over life and death. Relatives of the victims and survivors of torture all of a sudden sensed their opportunity to participate in this judicial process and to initiate similar proceedings. Like many of those who followed in their footsteps, they evolved from traumatized objects of totalitarian state power to trial subjects and political agents inside and outside the courtroom. During the painful trials, they reclaimed their memories, their political identities and, thus, their dignity.

Pinochet was released a year later due to his health condition. He was flown out to Chile and never brought to trial there. Nonetheless, his case continues to have an impact on the praxis of the legal human rights movement today that goes far beyond the individual case. Pinochet's arrest was not the result of a planned action. Rather, determined individuals and groups mobilized together to recognize and exploit the political momentum. They were gradually joined by exiles, victims, and professionals.

The British extradition proceedings against Pinochet drew upon evidence that human rights activists had gathered at great risk while the dictatorship was still in power: dossiers on individual disappearances and murders, complaints against detention, and so-called habeas corpus petitions in court. All these activities amounted to nothing during the dictatorship and, rather, seemed futile (and indeed were) when measured against the goal of saving the lives of the disappeared and detained. In the long run, however, these attempts and the decades of solidarity and campaign work provided the basis for the Spanish and British lawyers to justify the arrest warrant against Pinochet and later against the Argentine military.

The events in London were triggered by the filing of the first criminal complaint in Spain in 1996 by the lawyer Carlos Castresana, which was directed not against the Chilean dictator, but against the Argentine military dictatorship. He invoked the principle of universal jurisdiction—or the principle of world law—which, according to the Spanish laws of the time, allowed for the prosecution of crimes committed beyond Spanish borders that did not necessarily have to be related to the country. The tersely worded denunciation was directed against Argentine General Jorge Rafael Videla and others. Castresana's inspiration came not from studying law books—though, of course, he knew the law—but from the images of the mass demonstration in Buenos Aires on the twentieth anniversary of the military coup on 24 March 1976.

Gradually, survivors of the military dictatorship, Spanish lawyers working in solidarity, and exiled Argentine lawyers joined the proceedings and participated with witness testimonies, the presentation of evidence, and the filing of hundreds of cases. The Spanish judiciary began investigating the Argentine complex of cases, heard many witnesses, and issued the first international arrest warrant for Argentine military officers a little over a year later.

The Spanish judiciary only became interested in the Chilean military dictatorship later. It was mainly thanks to the energetic intervention of the then-investigating Judge Baltasar Garzón that Pinochet's temporary presence in London led to his imprisonment and the subsequent extradition proceedings.

A boom and its limits

Since the 1960s, transnational, cross-border activism had primarily relied upon publicly effective protest events and educational campaigns to mobilize international solidarity. But now this activism was enriched by a legal element. When all options in one's own country for addressing the most grievous crimes were exhausted, and when those same crimes still went unpunished, institutions beyond one's own state—such as regional human rights mechanisms, international courts, or national courts in third countries—were called upon.

Triggered by the successes in the Argentine and Chilean trials, a network of diverse groups formed in the early 2000s: survivors of state injustice elsewhere in the world, their lawyers, human rights groups from affected countries and regions, and international organizations such as Amnesty International and Human Rights Watch. After all, the Argentine and Chilean militaries were not just the subject of extensive investigations in Spain, but also in France, Italy, and Germany, and convictions in absentia were handed down. In addition, at the behest of other affected parties, legal proceedings were initiated addressing events in Congo, Rwanda, Israel, and China—in other words, against powerful human rights violators all over the world. In Spain and Belgium in particular, the judiciary was comparatively receptive and investigated numerous cases.

The years following the adoption of the so-called "Rome Statute" in 1998 were characterized by an optimism surrounding the International Criminal Court with its establishment of an international criminal justice system for international crimes.

Activists and lawyers from all over the world wanted to seize the opportunity to make their case. However, the requests, which in most cases were well-founded and justified in themselves, were insufficiently coordinated at both the national and transnational levels. As a result, the mobilization of political support for individual cases and for the exercise of mandates for global justice within the nation-state framework often failed. For example, after a few years, laws in Belgium and Spain—where many important trials had previously taken place—were retracted as a result of political pressure.

Due to these considerable setbacks, human rights organizations and jurists came to the conclusion, for strategic reasons, to initially only use legal means against less powerful individuals. First, a solid practice of international criminal law needed to be established at the national and international levels. Criminal proceedings against influential actors, it was argued, were too politically charged, and the proceedings too politicized.

This realization was reinforced by the research of Argentine legal scholar Máximo Langer, who demonstrated that in the late 2000s, over 1,000 criminal complaints were filed from the five Western European jurisdictions of Spain and Belgium, as well as France, the United Kingdom and Germany, against alleged human rights violators all over the world. Many of these were against members of powerful states, where it would have been legally possible to initiate criminal proceedings in European states—for example, for Russian war crimes in Chechnya or systematic torture by the USA in Iraq and Afghanistan. However, only slightly more than thirty cases involving crimes in African states, Yugoslavia, or Nazi Germany culminated in prosecution and judgment. According to Langer, international criminal law is applied when the danger of political and economic damage is low, i.e., primarily against members of weak states or against persons who have already left their positions of power. Powerful violators remain unchallenged. Thus, double standards prevail in international criminal law.

While many, also from within the human rights movement, regarded this as an unalterable fact, others fought against it: for example, starting in 2004, I myself was involved in several criminal complaints in Germany, France, Spain, and Switzerland against members of the Bush administration for systematic torture in Iraq's Abu Ghraib and in the Guantánamo prison camp. The complainants called for the same legal standards to be applied to powerful human rights violators as were demanded by US Chief Prosecutor Robert Jackson at the Nuremberg trials.

The proceedings against former US Secretary of Defense Donald Rumsfeld can certainly be seen as an example of "success without victory." Their express aim was to communicate to the world a thorough documentation of the systematic nature of the crimes of torture ordered and carried out by the political, military, and intelligence leadership of the United States, along with a comprehensive legal analysis based on this documentation. The complainants wanted to initiate investigations in Germany under the Code of Crimes against International Law introduced in 2002. However, this did not happen even after several attempts. Nonetheless, the criminal complaints stimulated jurisprudential and public debates in Germany and elsewhere, while attracting worldwide attention. As a result, a number of smaller goals were achieved: the norm of the absolute prohibition of torture, anchored both in international law and in many national statutes, was successfully defended discursively, at least in Europe. The defense strategy of former US President George W. Bush, according to which the acts of torture committed in Abu Ghraib could be attributed to individual "rotten apples"—i.e., low-ranking scapegoats—came to nothing. Instead, the responsibility of top military officers and politicians has since been substantiated in numerous articles and academic publications. The debate likely spurred subsequent legal efforts in a number of other countries by well-connected human rights organizations from North America and Europe.

For example, prosecutors in Munich and Milan issued arrest warrants for individual CIA personnel for their involvement in the CIA's extraordinary rendition program and, in particular, the abductions of German citizen Khaled al-Masri and Egyptian cleric Abu Omar in Italy. The illegality of the aforementioned program was implicitly established in several decisions of the European Court of Human Rights, namely in 2012 in the case of al-Masri against Macedonia and in other cases against Poland and Lithuania.

Several judicial inquiries took place in the United Kingdom regarding Ali Zaki Mousa, an Iraqi prisoner of war who was tortured to death. In several hundred cases, the United Kingdom paid compensation to the affected parties. In addition, the country was twice convicted by the European Court of Human Rights. The International Criminal Court's Office of the Prosecutor opened preliminary examinations into the matter at the beginning of the summer in 2014 following ECCHR's intervention, but then closed them in December 2020 on dubious grounds.

There was another interesting effect of the prosecution efforts in Europe: internally, the CIA warned several hundred affected employees about traveling to Europe and other regions where they feared criminal proceedings on torture could take place. Even President Bush himself, who was no longer in office at the time, refrained from taking a private trip to Switzerland that was planned for the spring of 2011 after he learned of a criminal complaint filed by torture survivors.

Not enough, but more than nothing.

Establishing a praxis: the Syrian complex of cases

The 2000s and 2010s saw the development of a consistent praxis for criminal proceedings based on the principle of universal jurisdiction in Western Europe, such as in the Syrian case-complex.

First of all, the widespread impunity for international crimes committed since the 2011 uprising in Syria is evidence that the institutions of the world community are not functioning as they should. The UN was unable to stop the mass killings in Syria, in part because numerous foreign states, including those with veto power in the UN Security Council such as Russia and China, were involved. Moreover, to date it has been impossible in both Syria and in the region to launch investigations into the Assad regime. Efforts to establish a UN special tribunal based on the example of Yugoslavia failed—as did the opening of investigations by the International Criminal Court's Office of the Prosecutor—because Russia and China vetoed them. Therefore, criminal proceedings in separate countries under the principle of universal jurisdiction remained the only option.

Thus far, proceedings against low-ranking suspects from Islamist organizations and the IS have been conducted in several Western European countries, not only on the basis of international criminal statutes, but often concerning terrorism.

Along with France, the Federal Republic of Germany plays the most active role in this arena. Based on the pro-international law provisions of the German Code of Crimes against International Law, a specialized department at the Federal Public Prosecutor's Office in Karlsruhe has been conducting extensive investigations on Syria and gathering intelligence on the situation there since the beginning of the uprising.

As a result of the criminal complaints filed by those affected, the proceedings gained new momentum over the course of 2017. The Syrian exile community in Germany, which is almost one million strong, contributed to this: Syrian and German human rights organizations presented the Federal Prosecutor's Office with three extensive criminal complaints with numerous witness statements from many torture survivors residing in Germany. Furthermore, original files with 27,000 photos of the corpses of people tortured to death were sent to the Federal Prosecutor's Office by the group centered around the military photographer, Caesar. The Federal Prosecutor's Office had these forensically evaluated with the aim of establishing findings on the causes of death and the patterns of perpetration. Human rights organizations then demanded that European and international arrest warrants be issued against high-level suspects who were not in the Schengen area.

Already for members of the Bush administration and the CIA, travel in Europe had recently been severely limited by the threat of prosecution under the principle of universal jurisdiction. In the case of the Syrian intelligence chiefs, the Federal Supreme Court—Germany's highest criminal court—identified an urgent suspicion of crimes against humanity. This legal categorization of state torture in Syria and the evidence and findings gathered as a result provide a solid basis for future proceedings with other European law enforcement agencies, international forums, and institutions even within Syria itself. The actions of individual nation-states, such as Germany and France, are strengthened by the fact that a separate Independent Commission of Inquiry has been established at the UN level, along with a hybrid entity—the so-called IIIM (International Impartial and Independent Mechanism)— that combines investigation and prosecution.

As early as two decades ago, such crimes against humanity would not have been investigated, let alone sanctioned. Therefore, the current proceedings prove that the principle of universal jurisdiction with the backing of the UN can be a limited, yet indispensable alternative to prosecution before an international tribunal.

While initially almost all criminal proceedings took place in the Global North, in the last decade something also happened in the Global South. In a historic trial in Buenos Aires in 2016, fifteen high-ranking former military officers were convicted of crimes against humanity in the context of the continent-wide intelligence operation Condor. Under the leadership of the United States, this operation consisted of a transnational cooperation between the intelligence services and militaries of the dictatorially-ruled states of South America to persecute opposition figures in the 1970s. The fact that not only individual soldiers and officers—but also generals—have now been convicted in connection with the transnational intelligence network must be seen as a breakthrough. The trial of the former dictator of Chad, Hissène Habré, represents the most important African case along these lines. Inspired by the success of the Pinochet case, survivors and their lawyers fought in courts in Chad, Senegal, Belgium, and the International Criminal Court for justice. In a historic trial that took place in a dedicated special court in Dakar, Senegal, Habré was finally sentenced to life imprisonment for—among other things—extensive torture committed during his rule beginning in 1982. Here, too, prosecution under the principle of universal jurisdiction before a Belgian court had already laid the foundation.

It remains conspicuous that perpetrators of sexual and gender-based violence enjoy the most widespread impunity before national and international courts. Although the legal prerequisites for prosecution of these crimes have long been in place, police authorities investigate these crimes insufficiently, while public prosecutors and courts shy away from indictments and criminal proceedings. Systemic violence is often relativized into unfortunate individual cases, whose prosecution, if it actually occurs, only targets individual perpetrators instead of those superiors who are ultimately responsible for the violence. For this reason, there have been very few trials that have addressed the endemic sexual violence perpetrated in almost all wars and situations of oppression. This makes the survivors of Japanese forced prostitution during the wars in Asia from 1931 to 1945 all the more deserving of credit for their perseverance. Admittedly, the sexual enslavement of an estimated 200,000 women was not addressed in the Tokyo War Crimes Tribunal, but the women pursued numerous legal, political, and artistic initiatives to get justice. Of particular note is the international opinion tribunal in Tokyo in 2000, which, after many years of preparation, provided an important impetus for academic reappraisal and legal policy debates. More recently, the survivors and their supporters have organized readings and demonstrations, and also erected statues to commemorate the fate of the women—most recently in Berlin in September 2020. The Japanese government demanded, mostly with success, that the statues be removed from the public space, thereby bringing further attention to the initiatives while at the same time demonstrating the continued ignorance around this issue to this day. These artistic interventions must be seen as successful.

Nevertheless, it can be stated that within the last twenty years—mainly at the behest of civil society entities—a judicial practice has emerged which would have been previously unthinkable and which at least partially cures an institutional deficiency within the UN.

Hopes disappointed: The International Criminal Court in The Hague

At the international conference in Rome in the summer of 1998, the proponents of the International Criminal Court (ICC) in The Hague were able to establish a largely independent court that would not be subject to the dictates of the UN Security Council, in addition to establishing an independent prosecuting authority. Within a few years, more than 120 states signed the statute, which went into effect in July 2002. However, to date, the permanent members of the Security Council—including the United States, Russia, and China—as well as other major states—such as India and Indonesia—have not signed the treaty. Other states which have been accused of human rights violations have also not signed. The jurisdiction of the court is therefore territorially limited, thus indicating both the strength of this approach—the creation of an international court with large support from the majority of states—as well as the weaknesses—the lack of participation of the most powerful states.

The court receives heavy criticism primarily because the formal investigations conducted there involve predominantly African countries, including Congo, the Central African Republic, Sudan, and Uganda. The first defendants and trials exclusively involved Africans. However, as accurate as this critical description of the state of affairs may be, the analyses fall short.

This is because three of the trials were referred to the court by African signatory states themselves, and two others—concerning Sudan and Libya—were referred by the UN Security Council. Thus, in these trials, it was not the prosecutorial authority from The Hague that made the selection. If one also takes into account that the vast majority of African states are signatories to the statute and that a large number of the international crimes committed in the last eighteen years were committed there, this also pushed back against the criticism.

It's true that the selection and handling of so-called preliminary investigation proceedings by the ICC's Office of the Prosecutor must be criticized. Nevertheless—and this is largely unknown to the public—preliminary examinations into the crimes of the USA in Afghanistan, additional international crimes in Colombia, Russia/Georgia, Ukraine, Nigeria, Honduras, South Korea, the Philippines, Venezuela, and Israel/Palestine have also taken place. Criticism flared up primarily around the handling of crimes committed by paramilitaries and state security forces in Colombia, which have only been "under observation" by the prosecutors in The Hague since 2006, even when the national prosecution authorities in Colombia have thus far failed to charge those most responsible, let alone convict any perpetrators for their actions.

In the case of the allegations of torture against the British military during their period of occupation in southern Iraq in the region around Basra, the former chief prosecutor Luis Moreno-Ocampo refused—in a manner that definitely warrants criticism—to open an investigation in 2006. However, in spring 2014, a preliminary investigation was opened by his successor Fatou Bensouda after the submission of numerous documents and records by nongovernmental organizations. The investigation was closed in December 2020 on questionable grounds.

The sharp criticism since 2012 of these practices of investigation and prosecution—alongside threats of withdrawal from the charter, in particular from Africa—has led to the clear discursive rejection of these double standards and this discrimination against African states. However, changes can also be observed in practice. This is evidenced, among other things, by the harsh reactions from the United States and other Western states to the decisions of the Office of the Prosecutor to conduct preliminary investigations into Israel/Palestine and Afghanistan, possibly investigations even involving US soldiers.

Business and human rights

It was not only the crimes of state and military leaders that were judged at Nuremberg. In fact, the Nuremberg prosecutors planned a second major tribunal against business leaders for the involvement of their companies in Nazi crimes. When this failed, prosecutors at least conducted follow-up trials against the owners and managers of the Krupp, IG Farben, and Flick corporations, the major industrialists of the Nazi regime. The economic trials accounted for one-third of all Nuremberg proceedings. However, as tensions between the Western Allies and the USSR increased, the prosecutors were forced to conclude the trials of the business leaders prematurely. This was because, in the eyes of the Western Allies, the old Nazi elites were needed for the reconstruction of the Federal Republic of Germany.

This part of legal history, which deals with criminal liability for corporate complicity in the context of war crimes, faded into obscurity during the decades that followed. Neither the UN tribunals for Yugoslavia and Rwanda nor the International Criminal Court have yet brought significant cases against economic actors—although many commentators agree that this would in principle be both possible and advisable.

Many of the conflicts currently under investigation in The Hague have economic origins, and Western actors are heavily involved in them. Consider the violent disputes over raw materials in eastern Congo. For years, local precious metal mines have been the cause of brutal clashes between various warlords and central government troops, as the mined raw materials are a welcome source of revenue. It would be legally possible to prosecute the managers of the foreign companies involved in these disputes for war crimes, as the mining of raw materials in conflict regions is considered the war crime of looting. The supply of weapons to paramilitary groups, the procurement of technical equipment or simply the financing of armed groups can be interpreted as aiding and abetting war crimes or crimes against humanity if the leading employees of international companies have the requisite specific intent. Nevertheless, for a variety of reasons, deeds of this kind have not yet been comprehensively investigated nor has anyone been charged.

As early as the late 1970s, lawyers in the United States were considering suing for damages for the victims of the massacre in Mỹ Lai, Vietnam. This planning was successfully implemented in 1980 in the case of the Paraguayan torture victim Jose Filártiga against the US-based Paraguayan military soldier, Peña-Irala. Following this landmark decision in the victim's favor, non-governmental actors initially successfully sued additional individuals who had participated in state injustice in the years that followed, such as Bosnian politician Radovan Karadžić, for damages for international crimes. Then, in the early 1990s, victims of corporate injustice in the United States sought reparations, such as in the cases of the oil companies Unocal and Shell for their activities in Myanmar and Nigeria, where opposition to oil production had been violently repressed by those states.

In 2009, for example, a lawsuit against the British oil company Shell by the relatives of Nigerian environmental activist and writer Ken Saro Wiwa—who was sentenced to death and executed after a political show trial—was concluded with a settlement in which Shell agreed to pay $15 million. In a follow-up case, however, the highest US court came to a corporate-friendly decision in April 2013. Transnational corporations from all over the world have historically mobilized politically on a massive scale against the application of the Alien Tort Claims Act. Nevertheless, the lawsuits led by non-governmental organizations in the United States have given impetus to similar proceedings and laws all over the world.

Dictatorship crimes and corporations

Inspired by the Nuremberg follow-up proceedings against business leaders, the lawsuits in the US, and the successful international criminal cases in the late 1990s, the involvement of corporations in international crimes came to the attention of European jurists—for instance, with the criminal charges I filed in 1999 against a Mercedes Benz manager for his involvement in the forced disappearance of a trade unionist in 1976 and 1977. Circumstantial evidence suggested that company management and the military had worked closely together in the suppression of workers' councils at the Mercedes plant.

Despite the lack of legal success of these charges, the proceedings against the manager and the company in Germany, Argentina, and the US proved that human rights activists can set their own course by using legal means. When Pinochet was arrested, the public was still so focused on the military that the political and social background of the repression was hardly taken into consideration. Legal institutions from Europe entered the scene as important agencies in the fight against the impunity of Latin American perpetrators. The criminal charges against Mercedes Benz, as well as Ford, made it clear that a significant percentage of those forcibly disappeared in Argentina and Brazil—along with the victims of additional human rights violations—were trade unionists and those within the labor movement. For standing in the way of the neoliberal restructuring of society, they were thus violently repressed with the consensus and participation of national, as well as transnational, corporations.

Unlike those affected individuals with a bourgeois background—such as journalists or lawyers—these workers had little access to publicity, to international solidarity, or to legal forums. The case of the disappeared Mercedes Benz trade unionist received a lot of attention in Argentina and Latin America, as well as in Germany, even if the proceedings did not ultimately lead to any resounding successes because of their particular difficulties (political considerations, more challenging evidentiary efforts in comparison to those of powerful state institutions). Nevertheless, in September 2020, in a similar case constellation addressing the military dictatorship in Brazil, VW do Brasil agreed to pay almost nine million US dollars in compensation to various funds, which were intended to benefit the workers who were harmed, among others.

More recent efforts by human rights organizations in association with peace policy advocate groups are directed against European exports of surveillance technologies to authoritarian regimes and dictatorships, such as in Bahrain, Iran, and Syria, as well as against the export of armaments to conflict regions. In this context, the Office of the Prosecutor at the International Criminal Court is currently considering opening investigations into European companies for aiding and abetting war crimes by delivering arms to Saudi Arabia that were used in the Yemeni civil war.

Legal responsibility in global supply chains in the textile industry

The current trend is for activists, affected parties, and lawyers to make more frequent use of transnational legal channels. Initially, the focus was on criminal proceedings against state officials. Gradually, legal actions also began to target economic actors and, increasingly, those from the West. But in North American and European courts, it is still primarily violations of political and civil rights that are fought against. In the Global South, on the other hand, it is not only individual rights but also collective economic and social human rights that are being demanded, which will be discussed later.

The fact that this issue only landed on the agenda of Western organizations at this late stage has to do with the paternalistic attitude already mentioned. Some also shy away from this fight due to the risks involved with suing powerful companies in their own countries. Legal efforts have also been hampered by business-friendly and anti-human rights legal codes and a lack of adequate legal structures. As a result, this fight for justice must move toward normative and institutional reforms.

Until now, lawsuits for violations of workers' rights in European and international forums have seemed impossible because—as a result of globalization—legal and economic responsibility has been outsourced from German textile sellers to South Asian producers. In this day and age, the textile industry is the emblem for the globalized value chains. Paradoxically, it was the man-made disasters of the Rana Plaza factory collapse in Bangladesh in April 2013 and the factory fire in Karachi, Pakistan, in September 2012 that provided a jumping-off point for both the political and legal debate in Germany. Since the protection of the rights to life and to bodily integrity are legally more pronounced than labor rights violations, a good example of what globalization from below is now capable of achieving developed out of this. After the great solidarity campaigns of the 1960s and 1970s and the movements of the late 1980s and 1990s criticizing globalization, networks began to form during the last two decades between those affected, lawyers from the Global South and the North, and human rights organizations.

In the case of the Rana Plaza factory, the prospects for legal action against the international buyers of the goods produced there were immensely more difficult because a large number of companies purchased from there. For this reason, the violations of occupational safety could not be attributed to a specific company in most cases.

The accusation of not having better safety controls at the production site was easier to prove in the case of the Ali Enterprises factory in Karachi, since the facilities are used almost exclusively to manufacture the products for the German clothing company KiK. Initially, there were no plans to take legal action against the German company, as it had already agreed to negotiate an appropriate compensation settlement. Immediately after the accident, with the support of a Pakistani trade union, the survivors and the families of the deceased organized themselves into a grassroots entity. This fact cannot be emphasized enough: trade unions are significant in every respect for such disputes, and without the existence of competent representation for those affected, the legal actions would have remained isolated.

After the negotiations failed from the point of view of those affected, they deliberated on a possible course of action in Germany. For reasons of principle, they decided—together with ECCHR—to file a lawsuit with a small number of plaintiffs at the Dortmund Regional Court for compensation for pain and suffering. The proceedings before the Dortmund Regional Court ended unsuccessfully for the plaintiffs because of the statute of limitations upheld by the court. However, the overall assessment is that the lawsuit helped to persuade the KiK Group to pay substantial reparations to the injured parties in 2016, with the support of the International Labor Organization (ILO) in Geneva as a mediator.

In addition, the startling, attention-grabbing events in Pakistan and Bangladesh were at the center of public discussions beginning in spring 2016, which coincided with the deliberations of the National Action Plan for Business and Human Rights. For the first time, a larger public in Germany took an interest in those who produce goods for the German market at high risk to their own safety. Federal Development Minister Gerd Müller of the CSU launched a political initiative—the so-called Textile Alliance—to oblige foreign companies producing in Bangladesh to adhere to certain standards.

The Dortmund court case, as well as similar cases in Brazil and South Africa, not only received general attention through articles in numerous publications and documentary films, a virtual replica of the Pakistani factory contributed to the greater visibility of the case. The London-based expert group Forensic Architecture proved, using the replica, that if the factory owner and the German buyers had observed all the safety standards, far fewer people would have been harmed and killed.

Since then, the legal community has also been engaged in controversial discussions, as this is the first case in which an attempt has been made to counter the outsourcing of responsibility along global production and supply chains by demanding compliance with due diligence obligations.

Once again, what is crucial is the complementary interaction between lawsuits related to individual cases, public advocacy for those affected, solidarity-based support against the systematic violation of labor rights, and the demand for human rights protection in law reforms. It is only because of these combined activities that the German Supply Chain Act could see moderate success in the form of legal obligations for larger companies that have production facilities worldwide.

A large sector of the business lobby is doing its best to resist any form of legal obligation, while some companies are openly embracing such initiatives, partly because the churches and trade unions, along with human rights actors, are taking a clearer stand in favor of them. Compared to the situation ten years ago, these are steps in the right direction. But there is still a long way to go before anything changes substantially for workers. This is also the case concerning the efforts to create a convention at the UN level to make transnational companies more accountable. Legal actions play an important role in this mixture of measures, as they present certain problems in a more sharpened and antagonistic manner, allowing those affected to articulate themselves as spokespersons in Europe without others speaking for them.

Collective law enforcement in India and South Africa

Laws are ordained by the Supreme Court in Washington, by the House of Lords in London, and by the German Federal Constitutional Court. Only the legal history of these metropole states is studied. The handbook of great jurists is comprised of men from Europe and North America. Legal proceedings concerning human rights violations in other parts of the world are less frequently reported and debated, both due to ignorance and because the legal systems there are often regarded as inferior to those in the West.

Yet, the last two decades have witnessed exciting developments in Latin America, Asia, and Africa.

South Africa enshrined economic and social rights in its constitution, as did Bolivia and Ecuador. Ecuador not only decreed the sanctity of environmental protection; it also went so far as to formulate *buen vivir*—the good and harmonious life in harmony with nature—as a constitutional principle. This notion reflects a new relationship between humans and nature, which grants the mother earth, Pachamama, her own rights and draws upon the cosmologies of the indigenous peoples. It opens up space for a political-economic model that extends beyond the Western credo of "development through growth and exploitation of nature."

Initially, this has not had much bearing on the actual situation for the people there: in South Africa, the social situation of the Black population is still precarious and formal political equality has not yet been followed by economic equality. The differences between rich and poor remain enormous. Natural resources continue to be exploited in Ecuador and Bolivia without regard for the new constitutional principles. Yet, many affected communities in South Africa are making use of the constitution in their struggles, and the newer constitutional concepts are providing an impetus for discussions among climate change activists around the world.

In addition, affected people in many countries in the Global South have initiated remarkable legal proceedings. In countries such as Mexico, Colombia, India, Pakistan, the Democratic Republic of the Congo, and Cameroon, land and participation rights are being asserted, while infrastructure projects and companies are being sued for human rights violations.

The oil companies Shell and Unocal paid out millions of dollars in settlements in US courts. In perhaps the largest environmental trial ever heard before the Supreme Court in Quito, Ecuador, the US oil company Chevron was ordered to pay $9.51 billion in damages in 2013 for environmental damage caused by oil production in the Amazon rainforests. This highlights the possibilities of legal action in the countries of the South, even if Chevron has so far managed to defend itself against the verdict.

Increasingly, affected people are also suing for collective economic and social human rights, which have been neglected in the West. For example, in India and South Africa, which are two countries with developed legal systems in the Anglo-American tradition and which therefore contain substantial opportunities for public interest litigation. In India, many social movements with strong memberships seek access through their lawyers to what is, on paper at least, progressive law. In addition to the rights guaranteed in the constitution, India's highest court is characterized by greater political independence than, for example, its counterpart in the United States that is dominated by party politics. However, the debate following the death of Justice Ruth Bader Ginsburg also makes clear that important political issues should not be left solely in the hands of small judicial bodies. Otherwise, democratic political change will be rendered impossible.

The Indian Human Rights Law Network (HRLN) and the People's Union for Civil Liberties (PUCL), with Colin Gonsalves (already mentioned in the prologue) as their lawyer, achieved worldwide success with the filing of several lawsuits on the right to food beginning in 2001. For the first time in history, a lawsuit in the public interest without an explicit mandate from the affected parties— so-called Public Interest Litigation—legally asserted the human right to food before the Indian Supreme Court. The HRLN lawyers argued that the constitutional right to life is violated when thousands of Indians die of hunger every year. The court followed their arguments, established the validity of the right to food as part of the right to life in the Indian Constitution, and mandated that the government provide nutrition programs for some 300 million people. Observers considered it a decisive factor that the case was supported by a broad social campaign.

Admittedly, this did not permanently eliminate hunger in India or its systemic causes, as left-wing groups have criticized. But the decision, in conjunction with social mobilization, noticeably improved the situation of millions of people. With this lawsuit before the Indian Supreme Court, a piece of global legal history was written. It demonstrated how the law can be used to enforce social human rights.

In the transnational struggles for the right to water and for those resisting the privatization of water, initiatives active in this field utilize the courts within their countries, in addition to educational means, mass mobilization, and direct action.

For example, the residents of a township near Soweto in South Africa filed a lawsuit against a private water company, the city of Johannesburg, and the minister in charge because a new water distribution system had been introduced in their town. The lawsuit was preceded by a political campaign that included demonstrations and the destruction of water meters. Legally, this campaign led to partial successes, insofar as the courts declared the forced introduction of the prepaid system unconstitutional and ordered the provision of a free minimum supply of water. However, the South African Constitutional Court overturned these rulings on the grounds that improving social conditions was the responsibility of the legislative and executive branches—but only within the framework of the available state budget.

The battle in the streets and legal discourse are thus by no means mutually exclusive. This is also visible in the example of the Bolivian city of Cochabamba, where the water supply was privatized as a result of pressure from the World Bank. The US company Bechtel was granted the concession rights and immediately raised water prices drastically. The inhabitants of the city mobilized against this selling-out of their commons. Violent clashes broke out between demonstrators and state forces, at the end of which the company was forced to withdraw. And this was not the only outcome: the right to water was then enshrined in Bolivia's constitution during the administration of Evo Morales and was even decreed as such by the UN General Assembly in 2010. This time, the indigenous people, who had been oppressed for centuries, were the winners. Even the 25-million-dollar lawsuit against the state of Bolivia before the ICSID arbitration court was withdrawn by the company under enormous public pressure in 2006.

The proceedings described here show how dynamically and creatively social movements in the Global South—together with their lawyers—use the law as a tool in the struggle for social human rights. Unlike many lawyers in the North, they understand human rights to be more than the civil and political rights to freedom of expression, freedom of the press, and protection against torture and murder. For them, political and social human rights are indivisible and must be demanded, no matter the forum or type of proceedings that are used—even when it is not fully possible to actually enforce these human rights legally. Frequently, proceedings in the Global South fail due to the limitations of legal norms and the political power relations that obstruct the enforcement of rights.

In the cases described, it can be seen that effective enforcement depends on legal rules, as well as on the possible avenues to sue for these rights. The appropriate legal elements of offenses are necessary to begin to grasp global economic activities and the human rights violations they cause.

This can be done, as in US tort claims or, as in the case of Indian and South African courts, with direct reference to international criminal law, international human rights covenants, or national constitutions. Similarly, civil or criminal liability statutes may be used, as is the case with lawsuits in continental Europe. In these cases, human rights violations are covered by the statutes of national law: torture and the right to bodily integrity are charged as severe bodily harm, and violations of the right to food and adequate housing are charged as private and personal property violations or offenses.

However, the success or failure of the proceedings described here does not depend solely on the implementation of human rights in national law, but also on the political situation. Such proceedings are still unusual today. This is because they challenge the neoliberal promise that economic activities regulate themselves in the interest of the common good and that global production and trade in goods bring positive effects for all. Lawsuits against companies confront us with the unpleasant facets of globalization because they give underprivileged, marginalized people a forum in which they, as legal subjects, may condemn wrongdoing. Segments of the public are therefore skeptical of such proceedings, describing them as sensationalism or as slander against supposedly honest merchants. Those given the task of judging the facts in the judiciary often belong to an elite class themselves and thus are not free of these preconceptions. They treat such cases accordingly. This skepticism is supported by the many legal rules designed to safeguard economic transactions. These ensure that the individual subcompanies within transnational corporate conglomerates are not responsible for each other and that managers are not liable for undesirable developments within subsidiary companies.

Whether in Europe, the United States, Latin America, Africa, or Asia, an open-minded political climate is needed for the lawsuits described here to succeed. It is not surprising, then, that progressive legal practices emerged in India with its democratic struggles in the 1980s and 1990s, in post-apartheid South Africa, and more recently in Ecuador. Ecuador and South Africa found themselves in the midst of social and political upheaval, and thus gravitated toward greater acceptance of social concerns and human rights. In India, until recently, there was a climate of openness toward addressing issues of hunger and justice.

Many organizations in the Global South are aware of the interaction between the political and legal spheres and therefore rely on other political strategies in addition to legal procedures, precisely because they want to influence the legal political climates of their respective societies in order to bring about social and legal change.

OUTLOOK

1. Argentina as a model for legal-political human rights work

A certain skepticism about strategic lawsuits undertaken by non-governmental organizations and their focus on litigation in court is justified, as non-legal forums are often underestimated. In contrast, the practices of the Argentine human rights movement can serve as a synthesis between the often-widespread naïve faith in the rule of law in Europe and any criticisms of this approach.

Argentina in the 1970s was the scene of one of the greatest crimes against humanity of the last century. Unlike other places afflicted by similar devastation, an effective and innovative human rights movement emerged there.

To this day, the Mothers and Grandmothers of the Plaza de Mayo stand at its center, an unparalleled organization comprised of family members of the estimated 30,000 disappeared. These relatives refused to be intimidated by the state terror which was also directed against them and, instead, organized and politicized themselves. Since 1977, they have made their rounds in white headscarves in the square in front of the presidential palace—the Plaza de Mayo—and lead every human rights demonstration in the front row. With their unconditional demands: "We want them back alive" and "Truth and justice for the disappeared," they set themselves an agenda based in realpolitik but, at the same time, also formulated a quasi-unfulfillable demand—a strong example of a concrete utopia. The latter, coupled with a unique patience and perseverance, was probably the reason why they resisted all attempts at co-optation or corruption and pursued their concerns undeterred for several decades.

Together with the children of the disappeared who became active later, they form the nucleus of a human rights movement that transforms private pain into collective struggle. The documentation of the crimes, their denunciations in front of the courts as well as the (world) public, and their public actions always went hand in hand.

The successful criminal trials, first in Spain and the rest of Europe and then in Argentina and Chile proper, were therefore not solely the result of legal procedures. It was actually the mobilization of the Chilean and Argentine human rights movements that played a decisive role. Human rights lawyers in both countries had already submitted all kind of legal appeals during the dictatorship, all of which were unsuccessful at the time they were filed, but which contributed to the careful documentation of the cases, as did the truth commissions established after the end of the dictatorship. In addition, numerous successes were achieved at the Inter-American Court of Human Rights, such as the truth trials arranged in Argentina.

The constant mobilization of civil society coupled with specific positive legal outcomes ultimately contributed to the aforementioned successes. The momentum was also right: at the time of Pinochet's arrest, the Democratic administration under Clinton promoted the case by releasing important documents. In Great Britain, Germany, and other countries, Tony Blair, Gerhard Schröder, and other social democrats were in power. In Spain, on the other hand, support for the South American proceedings was enlisted from deep within the circles of the Socialist Party, as the military's justification strategies were all too similar to the previous efforts in Spain to legitimize the Franco dictatorship's actions against its own leftist opponents.

American scholar Naomi Roht Arias described the Pinochet effect in Argentina and Chile as the reciprocal relationship between obstructed domestic remedies (local remedies) and the subsequent recourse to global remedies. With reasonable plausibility, she traced the domestic prosecution efforts, first in Chile and then in Argentina, back to the Pinochet arrest and the conviction of Argentine military officers by French and Italian courts, as well as to the arrest warrants and extradition requests ordered against them in Spain and Germany.

In Chilean courts, dozens of high-ranking representatives of the Chilean military dictatorship were sentenced to long prison terms, and in Argentina—especially after Néstor Kirchner came to power—more than 500 convictions were handed down against police, military, and secret service officials. Numerous other investigations are still ongoing in both countries.

In Argentina—unlike in neighboring Brazil, especially under President Jair Bolsonaro—a new incarnation of a military dictatorship is not an option, despite numerous existential economic and political crises. This is due, among other things, to the fact that the court proceedings and verdicts, as well as society's reckoning with the dictatorship's crimes, have been well received throughout the country. In Brazil, on the other hand, the amnesty and impunity of the military went unchallenged for a long time, and only much later were state investigations into the crimes of the dictatorship conducted.

The arts played a major role as a complement to the legal actions and the mobilization in the streets and squares. The works of photographer Marcelo Brodsky, for example, are about the reconstruction of memories. Drawing upon personal photos and objects, he processes the disappearance of his brother in a way that exemplifies his generation's reckoning with history, from the politicization of the late 1960s and early 1970s to the state's repression of the rebellion. In doing so, he creates the *mise en scene* of a collective memory.

During the times of impunity in the 1990s, a special form of action known as the *Escrache*—translated roughly as "bringing to light"—became popular: at the residences of well-known, high-ranking military officers, activists initially informed the neighborhood of their previous deeds and mobilized on certain days for a mixture of theater, art, and assembly. Artists such as the Grupo Arte Calle-jero engaged in street actions, for example, with imitation street signs on which they demanded *"Juicio y Castigo,"* or trial and punishment, for the human rights violators. With such interventions in public space, they made connections between the dictatorship, violence against the organized labor movement, transnational corporations such as Ford and Mercedes, and the authoritarian security policies of that time.

With "Archivo Caminante" (the Wandering Archive), artist Eduardo Molinari traces the historical lines of oppression in his projects, from colonial exploitation in Potosì—the city of silver—in Bolivia, to the military dictatorships of the twentieth century, to the current neoliberal economic model established by them. His work "The Soy Children" is particularly impressive: he portrays the genetically modified landscapes in the triangle of Brazil, Paraguay, and Argentina. He then tells of children who, at the edges of the fields sprayed with the pesticide glyphosate, acted as human flags to signal to the planes where to spray the chemical, and thus themselves became exposed to the poison.

In places like the Hotel "Bauen" in the center of Buenos Aires (which was occupied by the workers), the memorial site Parque de la Memoria, or the former torture center Ex-ESMA, political events, exhibitions, and performances on current topics still take place today. In addition, memory work is carried out as human rights violations and their causes are researched and documented. The activists do not allow the confrontation with the dictatorial past to be pursued in isolation as a closed chapter of history. Instead, they repeatedly draw correlations between the present and the past.

In May 2017, the newly elected neoliberal president Mauricio Macri wanted to intervene in the legal reappraisal of the dictatorship. Hundreds of thousands protested against it, showing how tenacious and capable of mobilization the human rights movement has become. Macri subsequently distanced himself from his proposal.

It is no coincidence that an important stimulus for the new international women's movement came from Argentina, where, in addition to young activists, numerous women of *Ni una menos* in Buenos Aires have been active against the military and against femicide. The Mothers and Grandmothers of the Plaza de Mayo, whose main objective was to come to terms with the crimes of the military dictatorship, today call out to the young women: "We recognize that we were feminists."

2. How transformative are legal actions?

For historical reasons, political and civil human rights are better when they are spelled out: they open up more robust legal possibilities than economic and social rights, which also have become codified and acknowledged. This is why they were the first to be claimed by non-governmental organizations and by those affected in the transnational criminal proceedings against Augusto Pinochet and the Argentine junta generals beginning in the mid-1990s. They had a major impact, which is not diminished by the fact that the conviction of the murderous military leaders by no means remedied the inherited legacies of these dictatorships, such as the elimination of many cadres within the labor movement and the glaring increase in foreign debt.

Despite multiple objective and subjective hurdles, economic and social human rights claims are being filed on a large scale, especially in the Global South, targeting transnational corporations in addition to nation states. Collective lawsuits and struggles have been successful, especially when politically waged and accompanied by political mobilization.

The legal responsibility of European individuals and institutions is also being addressed by numerous local and international groups regarding human rights violations at the EU's external borders, as well as at internal European borders. At stake in these cases is the struggle for what Hannah Arendt calls the most fundamental of all rights—the right to have rights—by those who have already crossed borders and entered territories that belong to what the European Union so euphemistically refers to as the "area of freedom, security, and justice." In two recent judgments, the European Court of Human Rights dismissed complaints against Hungary and Spain (for collective deportations) on grounds that raised fundamental doubts among many observers about the Court's role as a beacon for human rights.

States have taken the Court (and the inconveniences it causes them) more seriously in recent years and have tried to exert pressure on it in various ways. The election of judges has become more politicized than ever, and substantial influence has been wielded through threats of withdrawal and initiatives that weaken the substance of the Strasbourg rulings during the process of their implementation. Many court decisions are also highly controversial internally. Similarly controversial opinions are taking shape within these institutions, just as they have within society at large. Therefore, those who advocate for the human rights of those seeking protection should not rely on legal avenues alone. Political processes are always needed to help people obtain their rights. However, the question for human rights activists should not be whether we should fight for the right of migrants to have rights— there is no alternative to this. It is rather a question of how and with what expectations these legal disputes are conducted, which campaigns are supported within the public sphere, and how they can be complemented by other initiatives.

Thus, the content of the "Universal Declaration of Human Rights" does not become reality by being successfully claimed in court. This is because most human rights violations, especially structural abuses, are systemic. Without combating the power relations that produce them, they can hardly be overcome. However, the fragmentation and globalization of law can create new forums in which the power relations between actors are even more exposed than in the old arenas. There is a certain asynchronous aspect to this: in certain moments, law can be more progressive, opening up more possibilities than the real political and economic power structures currently allow for. Many normative standards carry within them such overflowing possibilities, whose open-endedness and potential could not have been anticipated by their creators.

The shortcoming of the human rights movement, as well as in legal actions, remains that the unjust economic order was put on the agenda too late and—when measured against its actual importance—is still being insufficiently considered. As a result, even when the basic structures of the global economy have been the cause of human rights violations, little has been done to disrupt them. The limits of legal action therefore often lie in the systemic causes of inequality: in exploitation, in poverty, and in climate change.

In *The Code of Capital*, lawyer Katharina Pistor states that capital rules through law. It relies upon a legal system backed by state power, a "combination of legal asset-shielding devices and the state's willingness to extend a helping hand to capital to preserve not only capitalism but social stability . . ."

Property law was not only the engine behind the bourgeois enthusiasm for (human) rights in the 18th century. It and other frameworks—such as bankruptcy law, credit law, contract law, free trade, and investment protection—are still the basis of the capitalist world economy today, as seen, for example, in the economic programs of the World Bank and the International Monetary Fund. One of the most important decisions—the Washington Consensus of 1990—enumerates the observance of property rights after trade liberalization, privatization, and deregulation of the economy. Only when these are secured and enforceable, does saving and investing in the respective states make sense.

The business lobby in politics and the legal system has consolidated its position over the course of the past several decades. In the US and like-minded countries—where even health insurance for all citizens equates to socialism in the eyes of elites (at least before the COVID-19 crisis)—such positions are held to be sacrosanct.

In recent controversies about the patent rights of medicines—namely, HIV generic drugs at the World Trade Organization (WTO)—the pharmaceutical companies have had to capitulate in the face of enormous public pressure. In principle, though, nothing fundamental has changed in terms of the primacy of private property over the public interest.

According to Pistor, the law produces inequality in the international financial system by "giving private actors in economic life a toolkit of rights ... with which they can forge their own fortunes (at the expense of others)." It "extended the notion of property rights from the right to use an object at the exclusion of others to protect asset holders' expectations to future returns." She describes law as a toolbox that opens up a wide range of possibilities for putting it in the service of private profit-making. "In principle, anyone can try their hand at this, but practically, those who can afford the best lawyers are most likely to succeed." The transnational space is shaped by contracts, she claims, and two legal systems dominate the structuring of global finance: English law and the law of the state of New York. That's also where the headquarters of the largest global banks and law firms are to be found. "But if you can choose your law, you can also set the terms on which you will remain loyal to a particular law." When in doubt, arbitration courts are called upon instead of state courts.

"The roots of capital's ability to rule by law run deep and lie in the emergence of modern rights as private rights," Pistor states. Does it even make sense anymore to invoke the law, and more specifically, legally standardized human rights, in the globalized world economic order with its increasingly powerful corporations and banks?

Even if a "human rights protection standard" is formulated, the laws and practices that Pistor is talking about are incomparably more robust. Property owners have the resources and access to justice at their disposal that indigenous village communities fighting dirty mines or power plants can only dream about.

For legal human rights work, this means that more is legally possible on the international terrain. Yet, radical asymmetries—especially the imbalance of resources between companies and human rights organizations—must always be taken into account. Pistor, too, still sees law as an important battleground in which communities need to "regain control over law"—as the only "tool they have to govern themselves." Just as the lawyers of capital have used the law for centuries—shaping and interpreting it to suit their interests, she argues—the code of law can be used "to empower others who have experienced the empire of law mostly from below: as losers in the battles over enclosure of land, knowledge, or nature," for example. In her work, she identifies a number of areas of law that do not strictly belong to the traditional field of activity of the human rights movement yet, but definitely should, in light of escalating developments. She goes on to outline the initial conditions of a difficult struggle, in which only by means of a conscious effort can a real transformation be secured. This is precisely what is at stake here.

In the face of the often-glaring imbalance of power, only a strategically skillful combination of legal, political, and communicative (for instance, artistic) means, delivered at the right moment, will have any chance of success. In the best case, artistic and legal interventions could make themselves stand out with more willingness to take risks and a little more courage to confront even powerful actors—just as Jacques Derrida once called for "changing the existing state of law" and "inventing new rights," even if they "always remain inadequate to" what he called justice.

Lawyers and human rights organizations will not be able to do this alone. This process will require very powerful political mobilizations—bringing together the movements of those affected, as well as those active in the institutions and the arts—to counteract the power imbalance just described.

6

Envisioning the Unimaginable and Opening Spaces of Possibility

It seems so self-evident when James Baldwin says it: "Not everything that is faced can be changed, but nothing can be changed until it is faced." That is, not every problem that is faced can be solved, but nothing will change unless an attempt is made.

Because history is open to all of us and to everything possible, and because we, as human beings, are continually in the midst of participating in "unimaginable" events, I insist that human rights represent a concrete utopia that is worth dreaming about and working toward. It is also necessary to defend them against the sceptics, but more about that in a moment.

In times of climate crisis, a pandemic, and authoritarianism, the present may carry dystopian features. But at the same time, activists, artists, and experts are breaking with established conventions to forge counter-models for the future, people are taking to the streets to demand their own rights and those of others, and human rights organizations have expanded their repertoire to include legal action.

Nevertheless, more is necessary, and more is possible! What this "more" could mean—namely, a substantive work program charged with new content, new constellations of actors, a new division of labor, new forms of media for human rights work—is something I would like to outline in the subsequent sections.

The end times of human rights vs. possibilism

While there is talk here of hope and the utopian potential of human rights, elsewhere human rights have been declared dead. It is not neoconservatives or Russian diplomats who proclaim such things; rather, it is voices supposedly from within our own camp. Critics, such as former Amnesty International employee Stephen Hopgood, proclaim the "end times of human rights" or the post-human rights era. For them, what they see as a consistent lack of success poses a problem.

Hopgood fears a decline in the importance of human rights within international relations because, in his opinion, the world power that has until now advocated for them, the US—and along with it, Western dominance—is losing influence to China. In addition, he suggests that the US itself has abandoned the project. For him, human rights as a secular, universal, and non-negotiable system of norms embodies the old model of Europe. However, Europe is no longer politically and economically powerful enough to spread its value agenda around the world. This leads him to state that the global legal system is now in decline because soon no state will have the power to globalize rules. He admits that human rights will likely continue to play a role, especially in the form of humanitarian aid, but he sees "symptoms of a deeper, creeping de-liberalization" in the rise of populist and authoritarian governments, to the detriment of human rights.

For Samuel Moyn as well, the concept of Western human rights organizations—exemplified by the cities of New York, London, Geneva, and The Hague—as well as by organizations such as Amnesty International and Human Rights Watch—has failed. According to Moyn, human rights grew in importance especially during the last decades, in which market fundamentalism was consolidated worldwide and economic inequality between and within states continued to increase. Moyn sees a way out of this, though: human rights activists must free themselves from the neoliberal grip and revive the dream of equality in theory and practice. Only then, he argues, can the ideal of human rights extricate itself from the unacceptable fate of a world becoming more humane in parts, but which is simultaneously experiencing a sustained increase in inequality.

Hopgood and Moyn's approaches are contradictory. They accuse Western human rights actors of being too fixated on their issues and methods, but they themselves focus their gaze only on the Global North, ignoring activities in and cooperation with the Global South. After all, key actors from these regions helped to build the institutional human rights system post-1945. Since then, new impulses have come repeatedly from India, South Africa, and Latin America. In addition, the language of human rights has become entangled in countless local and regional initiatives and movements around the world, and has currently produced a whole generation of young lawyers who stand up for human rights everywhere, not just in the courtroom. In this way, the law—what was previously conceived exclusively as ruling knowledge—is becoming more and more democratized.

This is not the only reason why the American political scientist Kathryn Sikkink vehemently disagrees with these skeptical analyses. According to her, their view of history and their facts are incorrect. Using empirical facts and data, she traces global trends in women's rights, hunger, and the death penalty. As a result, she demonstrates in writings such as *Evidence for Hope* that in comparison to the situation a few decades ago, there have been notable improvements.

Progress, however, should not be measured against an ideal state. The critics have an ideal in mind—a perfect state that will never be reached. Such an approach can only fail. And because they then become disillusioned, they become extraordinary pessimists that criticize human rights institutions very harshly. This pessimism can undermine people's will to bring about change. In any case, one cannot simply conclude that, because norms have been breached, the laws that were violated have now become invalid. For this reason, the human rights movement must counter those attempts to declare the concept of human rights a failure and to delegitimize the concept by pointing the finger at the miserable realities that remain unchanged.

Sikkink points out that for human rights, progress is primarily the result of activism and struggles. In this sense, her thinking aligns with possibilism, an approach developed by US economist and social scientist Albert O. Hirschman, who was an exile from Nazi Germany. According to him, the focus should be on what is possible and not just on what is probable. If people believe that the situation is hopeless, they are no longer in a position to fight for improvements.

Thus, the boundaries of what is perceived as possible must be expanded. Possibilism is important because people who believe in change can open up spaces of possibility and—sometimes—enable the possible to become real. That's why Hirschman was less interested in rules than in exceptions. He proposed a way of approaching the social world that privileges the unique over the commonplace, the unexpected over the expected, and, indeed, the possible over the probable. This is precisely why we're talking about unimaginable histories such as the Haitian Revolution or, on a smaller scale, the arrest of Pinochet and the reappraisal of the Argentine dictatorship.

This brings the concrete utopia of human rights back into focus. The human rights declarations, after all, neither delineate a real state that has already been achieved, nor do they declare how things—in a quasi-automatic fashion—will be from now on. Rather—whether after 1789 or 1948—they pushed the boundaries of what was perceived to be possible. Knowing that we cannot measure our actions against the end point of an ideal that cannot be achieved anyway—and, therefore, should not be frustrated by temporary failure—it is necessary to continue to stand up for freedom and equality and to enlist others to fight for these demands. The declarations provide the normative basis for us to demand more in the future than has so far been achieved.

We must do this without being naïve, of course, because the current challenges to human rights are real and not to be underestimated. We are in a period of profound transition. In times of climate crisis and during this pandemic, human rights activists can no longer go on with business as usual. In this spirit, I would like to invite discussion about the following proposals for new content, for a different division of labor, and for new methods.

A decolonial, feminist, and ecological approach to the social question

The Universal Declaration of Human Rights and the treaties that followed it represent a potential cornerstone of the concrete utopia of human rights. They offer a rich treasure trove of freedoms, of economic and social rights, and of individual as well as collective rights—a trove which is still waiting to be mined. However, the perception of the possible must still be heightened for many more people than before, through acts of disruption, as well as through educational, performative, and even emotional means. This is one important reason why we also need the arts.

However, this substantive program can be historically, thematically, and geographically enhanced—as well as sharpened along currently significant lines of conflict. This is why human rights work must always return to the "social question"[2] and the enduring inequalities that lie at its root, while reinventing itself through decolonial, feminist, and ecological interventions.

Decolonization—the long-overdue reckoning with colonial realities and their absolute antithesis to human dignity and human rights—must become a genuine human rights project. Large portions of European colonial societies continue to behave ignorantly towards the historical injustice and devastation of colonialism. Historical awareness can be advanced through museums, through discussions on the renaming of streets and colonial monuments, through education, through communication, and through artistic forms.

It is thus desirable for established human rights organizations—especially those within the legal community—to address their own shortcomings: for example, by examining the role of law in the legitimation of colonialism. In places where it is still possible today, those directly affected and their descendants should be supported in pending criminal and damage compensation proceedings. Initiatives for intergenerational justice—for comprehensive reparations for the affected populations and peoples such as the claims of the Herero and Nama against Germany for the historic genocide committed by the German Reich in what is now Namibia—should finally

2   The social question (in German: "soziale Frage") means certain evils and grievances affecting the wage-earning classes, and calling for their removal or remedy. The term "socialism," used from the 1830s onwards in France and the United Kingdom, was directly related to what was called the social question.

be taken up by those committed to the enforcement of human rights.

So far, most organizations have shied away from this domain. But decolonization also means coming to terms with the legacies and deformations of colonialism, hence the fight against postcolonial injustice. One way or another, access to land, resources, and cultural assets for those once dispossessed must be fought for, be it through individual or collective lawsuits, though the creation of just laws, or through the "New World Economic Order," which was brought into play by the newly independent states in the 1950s. A more equitable world economy must be organized so that all people have access to the necessities of life and so that these are justly allocated in accordance with their human rights. European states must reconceive their approaches. At the international level, they must act in the global (and not only in their own) interest.

The decolonization of North-South relations also requires a different kind of cooperation between human rights organizations (and others) from the Global North and those from the South: namely, one that is less hierarchical than at present. In addition to such concrete concerns, colonial history can be employed as a "kaleidoscope" to view the current conditions of today. The Black Lives Matter movement demonstrates this by tracing the current prevailing racism back to its historical formation as scientifically based racism that extended into all areas of society.

Feminism also presents us with a holistic picture of the world. As younger feminists in particular have stressed in recent years, feminism is not just about group-specific concerns. Rather, feminism essentially amounts to a global indictment of neoliberal capitalism, the struggle to abolish the opposition between the political and the private, and the continuous fight against the discrimination of women, as well as LGBTQ groups.

The climate crisis can also be used as a kaleidoscope. Sectors within traditional environmental protection groups paint a colonial picture of untouched nature and of nature reserves and of their need for protection against humans and civilization. To this end, they often go so far as to demand the expulsion of indigenous communities from their ancestral territories, the only guardians of the environment and biodiversity in many places.

Those with an internationalist bent within the climate and ecology movements have promised to stand up for climate justice. They recognize that the old industrialized countries and corporations—especially fossil fuel companies—bear a disproportionate share of responsibility for the current calamity. And they emphasize that people in different parts of the world are affected very differently by climate change.

Thus, decolonial, feminist, and climate activists have arrived at the demand that only a comprehensive change in the prevailing economic system can bring an end to the exploitation of nature, of women (especially with regard to the kinds of labor historically imposed on women), and the formerly colonized. These are the forms of exploitation that classical Marxism and the political formations based on it largely ignored, both analytically and politically. These dimensions—taken together with the social question—delineate the scope of a comprehensive human rights program that includes the actual overthrow of systems of exploitation in which humans subjugate other humans.

However, human rights demands should not be exclusively directed at states. States should of course not be released from their responsibility to uphold human rights, especially the rights of the people living in their territory or threats to human rights emanating from their domain. But the historical focus on political and civil rights has led to a state-centered emphasis within the human rights movement. This must be overcome, for example, by holding transnational corporations responsible for human rights violations and the climate catastrophe. More recent developments, such as the role of the financial sector and the effects of artificial intelligence, also need to be addressed in terms of human rights. And here, it is worth returning to Katharina Pistor and her call to oppose the legal code of capital as expressed in current property, contract, bankruptcy, credit, or commercial law. The relevant economic and political developments therefore require continuous analysis: neither the content nor the methods of human rights work are predetermined or timeless but, rather, must be constantly adapted.

Towards a new division of labor

Working on such a broad program calls for new actors and new combinations. Individuals and organizations working specifically on human rights locally and globally must be joined by others, namely social movements, including those not explicitly dedicated to human rights, in addition to interdisciplinary experts from all regions and fields.

But how then to keep track of the already confusing terrain and how to organize a meaningful division of labor? The threatening disintegration of all these efforts into "particularisms" can certainly not be counteracted by proclaiming a new International or something along those lines. Apart from the previous limitations and political mistakes of the old International, this would be totally inappropriate for the current constitution of diverse historical, geographical, and issue-related struggles. Colombian human rights activist César Rodríguez Garavito therefore proposes that the field be understood as an "ecosystem" rather than as a unified movement or institutional architecture.

In such an ecosystem, the major international institutions and organizations, such as Amnesty International and Human Rights Watch, play an important role. Their competencies, experience, connections, and resources can be built upon. Amnesty International's global mobilization capacity and reputation, in particular, could provide a starting point for the efforts outlined here.

The aforementioned human rights organizations have denounced abuses over the past decades and achieved success in doing so. This includes "naming and shaming," i.e., naming those responsible for the human rights violations in question. This generates public political pressure, as it did during the campaign against the Chilean military dictatorship after 1973. In addition to this, tangible sanctions are often demanded against individuals, governments, or other entities that are believed to be responsible on the basis of the carefully researched reports by suprastate investigative bodies or Human Rights Watch. This can lead to particular sanctions, such as bans on entry or the freezing of accounts.

However, apart from their questionable consequences, these sanctions can only be enforced if there is unity or if the strong states stand behind them. Moreover, in practice, these sanctions are often applied only against other human rights violators and not against those from within their own camp, especially those from powerful states. Thus, they are instrumentalized by Western and other powerful states (groups) and as a result, are sooner or later discredited. In a multipolar world, powerful states such as Russia, India, and China can hardly be dealt with by such means. Furthermore, due to the multitude and, above all, the continuity of the human rights violations committed, it is simply not possible to respond with multiple reporting and sanction mechanisms for all situations in the same way.

Reporting on human rights violations, and the tactic of naming and shaming, have helped to establish a necessary condition for change. However, these approaches are not sufficient. The more complex interrelationships and systemic and structural causes of human rights violations still need to be analyzed and understood, still need to be communicated and, most importantly, still need to be addressed. This is where it gets difficult.

Currently, even insiders think there is an overabundance of reporting on almost every human rights issue in the world. Sometimes, the overall goal of all these reports and campaigns remains unclear. Who is to be made aware? Who is to be then mobilized to do exactly what? Which audience is expected to react to all the grievances highlighted and how? Too often the reports exhaust themselves in ritually replicating traditional methods that may have been successful in the past. A rhetoric of simplification and reduction of complexity is often adopted, and it is true that this triggers feelings such as pity in the short term. But how are these unstable, transient feelings to be translated into action?

Large international non-governmental organizations should not have a monopoly on human rights work. In the future ecosystem of human rights, others should be heard more often and more prominently. This includes affected people and their communities, as well as independent experts.

The different operational logics and roles of the respective actors should be discussed and accepted. Funding—including access to resources and the privileges of individuals—should be clearly identified and discussed in order to deal with contradictions and ambivalences in an open and transparent manner. This also requires breaking down the postcolonial, paternalistic structures of human rights work. It should not be the case that those who have the resources determine the agenda for virtually everyone else. This demand in particular is extremely difficult to discuss, let alone implement.

Many actors cling to the dripping tap of a few donors and would rather please them than criticize them. The dependence on these few is so great that the changes in strategy of large foundations based in London or New York can threaten the existence of those organizations funded by them. In any case, organizations should work more closely together instead of seeing themselves as competitors for dwindling resources.

Nowadays, it is sometimes more a matter of who works on which topic faster and in a flashier manner, as this ensures attention, than what is more beneficial to the cause. In fact, the cause would benefit more from a coordinated, collaborative process with multiple perspectives and with mutually agreed upon approaches. The interplay between those who confront the parties responsible for human rights violations, those who engage in mediation, and those who appeal to and engage in diplomacy could be better organized, while still avoiding mutual reproaches. We would also cover more ground if we stopped pitting local efforts against global efforts, or pitting the concerns of the so-called culture wars against deeper social questions.

What is needed is a new division of labor and better forms of cooperation. The linking of heterogeneous struggles could be achieved, at least discursively, through the concrete utopia of human rights. In contrast to other necessary and important concepts of struggle, such as global solidarity and universal emancipation, this notion has the distinct advantage that it gives normative guidance in many fields and that these norms are, at least partially, enforceable in concrete disputes. However, they do not represent a political project in the proper sense but, rather, only a basis for argument, as well as a basis for (legal) actions and interventions. This new division of labor and its political concepts must be coordinated in detail among those actively involved in the human rights movement. In this context, the current situation, dominated by multiple crises, requires both compromises and an unconditional commitment to fundamental change—one of the many contradictions that must be straddled in a global and complex world that is rapidly converging on itself.

Civil society activists should heed the words of Michel Foucault at a press conference in 1981:

> We are only private people here who have no other claim to speak of and to speak together about than a certain common difficulty in enduring what is happening...One must reject the division of tasks that is so often proposed to us: for the individuals to be outraged and to speak, for the governments to reflect and act...The right of private individuals to intervene effectively in the field of politics and international strategies. The will of the individual must inscribe itself in a reality on which the governments seek to reserve the monopoly, this monopoly that must be wrested from them anew step-by-step, every day.[3]

---

3   Michel Foucault, Den Regierungen gegenüber: die Rechte des Menschen, in: Christoph Menke / Francesca Raimondi (Hrsg.), *Die Revolution der Menschenrechte* [*The Revolution of Human Rights*], Berlin 2011, S. 159 – 160.

Therefore, the interaction between local and global actors—as well as the interaction between institutional actors and those operating outside institutions—should be rethought and practically reconceived. The existing structures of normative human rights and the people who stand up for them must therefore be defended and expanded. At the same time, however, the old structures should be broken open in order to recharge the substantive program of human rights, as well as the arsenal of its forms of struggle. This means that work must be done both with and against these institutions. The relationship to the institutions must be determined anew in each case.

Flexible action from all extra-institutional actors can lead to cities like Barcelona or Palermo declaring themselves safe havens for refugees while also standing as pioneers of new housing policies, However, self-criticism and critiques of power should not fall victim to short-term pragmatic considerations.

Thomas Gebauer of Medico International, for example, argues for a "multilateralism from below." In addition to the redistribution of resources in the spirit of solidarity, there is also a need to redistribute decision-making power. Global institutions could provide for the "transnational regulation and provision" of resources, whose applications would be decided upon "in democratically constituted self-administrations." This is especially important in light of the looming battles over the distribution of vaccines.

In no way should an incrementalist politics or a pragmatic stance supporting human rights within institutions be discredited. In these times of increasing authoritarianism, one stance cannot function without the other, for example, when people are in prison or must go into exile because they are threatened with great harm. Then, it is a matter of fighting for the existence and the dignity of the people affected and of maintaining or establishing the basis of all further struggles—the right to rights. But even with such concrete and pragmatic actions, one should not lose sight of utopia, as it enables actors and actions to push boundaries and help activists demand more than seems possible, leading them to publicly and loudly take steps toward progress together.

However, without people gathering in the squares and streets, no plan will work either. Partially liberated territories like Chiapas, Mexico—self-governed by the Zapatistas and indigenous communities—represent this fact. And the largest mobilizations of recent years by feminists, Fridays for Future and, most recently, Black Lives Matter have also made this clear, as did the 2011 Arabellion and the Occupy movements in Madrid and elsewhere.

For Judith Butler, the assembly of bodies in public spaces "[o]ver and against an increasingly individualized sense of anxiety and failure...asserts a plural and performative right to appear" and expressively makes "a bodily demand for a more livable set of rules." The communality of the situation is manifested and the individualizing of morality is contested.

The French writer Guillaume Paoli describes this with reference to the movement of the yellow vests: those previously invisible from the periphery of the production process came from the hinterlands and stirred up the country, occupying non-places such as traffic circles or supermarket parking lots, and transformed the wasteland into an *agora* because they met and talked to each other there.

So, this is also about feelings, such as recognition, respect, and dignity. But is also about powerlessness and frustration. The national trepidation about the presence of racists and right-wing extremists in the German parliament could be broken open because in May 2018 about 70,000 people spontaneously demonstrated in Berlin against a march of 4,000 right-wing extremists in the center of the city. A few months later, in October, 250,000 people came together under the programmatic motto "Indivisible" which was meant to symbolize the diversity of those gathered. The struggle for freedom—for refuge and migration—must no longer be allowed to be played off against the demands for equality and the welfare state.

The images of the Black Lives Matter demonstrations after the murder of George Floyd in May 2020—which took place not only in all major cities in the US but also in many European cities—have also been influential and motivating.

The human rights movement in the narrower sense, especially the internationally active organizations, could liberate human rights from its reputation of being a purely middle-class, elite project with a historically and substantively charged program of work. It could be decolonial and feminist in word and deed—with a new DNA that is critical of power. They will need support from the young, global mass movements and the local and regional groups—organizations and movements on all continents that are fighting for more just conditions, whether by invoking human rights or not.

There is no question that human rights, as understood here, offer enormous argumentative potential and that everyone must take up the struggle for law and justice with whatever particular content, methods, and forms work for them. However, this argument could be better communicated to the many who do not see human rights as their own project. In such a new formulation, the path would be open for concrete work on the utopia of human rights. When people are threatened by state or para-state violence or are unjustly imprisoned, tortured, or executed, quick and pragmatic reactions are necessary. Such defensive mechanisms have been developed in recent years also in concert with institutions, including states that maintain openness to certain concerns and issues, whatever their reasons for doing so may be. In this context, particular reference can be made to transnational regimes, such as the human rights courts and the various mechanisms of the UN. These concrete starting points include the legal actions mentioned above—a significant portion of which are dedicated to the defense of bodies and of spaces under threat (shrinking spaces). Not every situation requires that we go beyond ourselves or that we address foundational systems, but within the mosaic of the human rights movement, the arts and the notion of the forum have the potential to enrich us greatly.

Art and forensis

If one is to discuss new approaches to championing human rights, one has to talk about the arts. Here, I will take the liberty of being selective and only address some of the media and art forms—such as photography, literature, documentary film, and docufiction—that have always concerned themselves with historical and current human rights problems. It is probably no exaggeration to say that "engaged art" has become an important part of the human rights scene and has also enriched it. As a result, the discourse around human rights has become more profound, emotional, historical, and intersectional, opening up new approaches, as well as generating new actors and coalitions.

Works of art such as Francisco de Goya's *Distasters of War*, Ernst Friedrich's book *War Against War*, Erich Maria Remarque's novel *All Quiet on the Western Front*, Karl Kraus's *The Last Days of Mankind*, and Stanley Kubrick's film *Paths of Glory* emphasize an anti-war stance and convey sensual impressions to those of us born afterwards that go beyond factual descriptions. Gustave Courbet's paintings, Käthe Kollwitz's woodcuts, and Giuseppe Pellizza da Volpedo's *The Fourth Estate* helped shape the struggle for the dignity of workers. Paul Celan, Primo Levi, Ruth Klüger, as well as Imre Kertész sought to find words for an event that is beyond comprehension. The discussion of France's war crimes in Algeria would have been unthinkable without Gillo Pontecorvo's film *The Battle for Algiers*. Countless jazz songs like Billie Holiday's *Strange*

Fruit, Christian McBride's concept album *The Movement Revisited*, or angry hip hop songs like Run the Jewels' latest work denounce the murderous racism in the US and convey a historical understanding of resistance against it, although in very different ways and directed at very different audiences.

Even this brief list highlights the variety of artistic forms and expressions through which human rights issues can be processed, as well as the different effects these artworks can have: from documentation and clarification to exposure and accusation, to the search for clues and the furnishing of evidence, to the communication of different perspectives, to art as a practice of empowerment, to the (re)construction of memory and identity, to the triggering or disruption of feelings such as empathy, shame, and anger, and to the development of one's own language. Recent research projects such as "Artivism" by Lausanne professor Monika Salzbrunn deal with the carnival in Viareggio, the fashion scene in Genoa, as well as comics and graffiti in Los Angeles. Activist groups, such as the Center for Political Beauty, he Yes Men, and the Peng collective, publicly attack corporations and governments with installations, performances, and videos, a mixture of political activism and action art.

What seems important here is to recognize under what circumstances free or applied art can be considered an intervention, whether by standing on its own or in concert with other approaches.

The photos of war correspondents of Vietnam, which are today appreciated as a comprehensive artistic body of work, informed people all over the world about the war-mongering of the United States, as well as helping to fuel the protest against it. The photos taken by Eddie Adams from 1968 showing the Saigon police chief executing a Viet Cong man, Nguyễn Văn Lém, with a bullet to the head or the images of the naked nine-year-old, Phan Thị Kim Phúc, running out of her village in tears after a napalm attack taken by Nick Út were reference points for public debates in the US and the rest of the world. The definitively non-artistic photographs of the naked and tortured Iraqi prisoners from Abu Ghraib also acquired a similar status. The torture scandal was triggered in the summer of 2004 by these pictures of US soldiers. The photos became a worldwide symbol of misguided US policy.

The photographs and their incorporation, for example, in the paintings of Fernando Botero, served to generate a historical incision. There is a before and an after, which the purely textual depictions could not achieve. But the photos do require verification and contextualization. On the one hand, images can be technically falsified in ever more subtle ways or taken out of context. At this point, everyone is aware of the effects this can have. Often, images only display a cross-section of a more complex event, while more subtle forms of the use of violence by states, for example, remain hidden. On the other hand, illustrated books such as *Vietnam Inc.* by Philip Jones Griffiths also illuminate the war machinery behind the fronts. Errol Morris' documentary *Standard Operating Procedure* tells the story behind the Abu Ghraib photos, which were initially seen by then-US President Bush as nothing but evidence of the excesses of individual soldiers. The methodology of the systematic torture committed by the United States after September 11, 2001 only becomes clear through additional media such as Morris' film or reports by human rights organizations.

The role of photography has changed enormously due to the democratization of the medium by digitalization, by the fragmentation of the public sphere, and by the rise of social media. The pictures of corpses taken by the Syrian military photographer with the alias Caesar document the killing of tens of thousands of members of the opposition by the Assad government, as well as the system behind it. They now also serve as evidence in the first trials against the perpetrators. Nevertheless, the pictures did not have the same effect as the Vietnam photos. Rather, they created a feeling of powerlessness, presenting stories that are hard to explain. Due to their sheer number, they overwhelm the viewers, triggering general horror but not global outcry.

Moreover, the display of maltreated bodies is in itself controversial in many respects. In his essay *Decolonizing Camera*, curator Mark Sealy highlights the importance of image politics in the context of the hegemonic colonial exercise of violence and calls for the decolonization of the camera. The survivors of Abu Ghraib were not asked for consent before their faces were broadcast around the world. Nevertheless, if the photographs had not existed, much less resistance would have been generated.

With this in mind, Susan Sontag poses the fundamental questions of how meaningful and how politically effective it is when the suffering of others is put on display. She calls for "reflection on how privileges are located on the same map as their suffering, and may—in ways we might prefer not to imagine—be linked to their suffering, as the wealth of some may imply the destitution of others...a task for which painful, stirring images can supply only an initial spark."

How much closer together artistic and human rights interventions have come in the meantime can be seen in the theatrical tribunals of recent years, as well as in the concept of "forensis." Artists use the specific setting of court proceedings—the presence of all the participants at the same time in one place—as dramatic staging for confrontation and its intensification. The recent tribunals represent stagings of stagings: Russell's opinion tribunals were already only a substitute for real court proceedings, but at least with their collection and presentation of evidence, for example, on the Vietnam War or Japanese forced prostitution during the Second World War, they came very close to constructing the conditions of real proceedings. The Berlin House of Bartleby with its Capitalism Tribunal and the Argentine Alicia García-Herrero with her tribunal against neoliberalism go so far as to transplant their political accusations entirely into the theatrical cosmos, rarely referring to valid or desirable norms.

With the Congo Tribunal beginning in 2015, the dramatist and director Milo Rau staged a global event that took place in multiple locations, staggered over time. It was performed in Congo, then in Germany, and later in Switzerland, initially on the stages of packed auditoriums, and then finding an even larger audience as a film documentary about the Tribunal's sessions in both countries. By presenting many diverse perspectives and cleverly sequencing them, Rau was able to recreate the interactions in the various performances. The continuous involvement of the participants consistently heightened the level of discussion and thus heightened the overall impact of the project. In the open formats of Rau's theater tribunals—to which he invites very different personalities and offers them a forum—criticism and reflection are also woven into the performances themselves.

The London group Forensic Architecture offers an exciting approach with their concept of "counter-investigations," dedicating themselves to the creation of alternative modes of investigation. In recent times, the term "forensic" only referred to the judicial or criminological use of techniques in the fields of medicine, psychology, and other sciences to establish evidence. The group's director, architect Eyal Weizman, aims to revive the concept of the Roman forum as a multidimensional space for politics, law and economics. The group uses interdisciplinary research methods to investigate human rights violations and makes its findings and expert knowledge available to affected individuals and non-governmental organizations for the purpose of filing lawsuits. The aim is not only to produce a deeper understanding of complex interrelationships for a wider audience through the visual presentation of scientific findings, but also to illuminate the relationship between truth and falsehood.

The group re-enacted the NSU murder of Halit Yozgat in an internet café in Kassel in April 2006, thereby invalidating the version of events reported by an intelligence agent who was present at the crime scene and claimed not to have seen or heard anything concerning the shooting. Forensic Architecture is about approaches toward truth. They rarely provide their own versions of the facts under investigation but, rather, deconstruct state narratives. In so doing, the group prepares its work with media and artistic means in such a way that it can be addressed in public: the original forum. It is remarkable how all available visual and audio recordings of the events under investigation are tracked down and compiled, and how by combining them with architectural models a much more comprehensive picture emerges.

In this way, they escape the dilemma of photographers and lawyers, who can often only shine a spotlight on specific features of a complex, multi-layered event, while the systemic big picture is in danger of being lost. The interdisciplinary cooperation between forensic experts, journalist groups, and NGOs provides an exemplary approach to addressing human rights violations. In addition, Forensic Architecture brings cultural and political dimensions into the legal sphere by submitting the results of their work to court proceedings where possible, and by informing parliaments and the public along the way. In this way, they combine artistic and legal interventions.

The inclusion of artistic forms in human rights work and of human rights issues in art does not always do justice to the inherent logic and language of each respective field. Human rights organizations have been urged by their sponsors not to present themselves too verbosely and, rather, to make use of images for a more comprehensible external presentation of their work. Often photographs have been used in this way for mere illustration, or as decoration or ornamentation to supplement the hard facts in reports on human rights issues. Documentary filmmakers construct narratives that center around a hero or heroine because this can make stories easier to tell, as well as enhancing the "marketability of the product" by bringing in the corresponding human touch. In such cases, white lawyers or journalists are often placed in the foreground to make them appear as "saviors." With this, in opposition to postcolonial critiques, the politics of (humanitarian) aid are promoted. The documentary filmmaker feels more important because he or she can claim to be involved in real events of significance, while for the human rights activist, his or her significance is perceived in a more glamorous context beyond his or her own sphere.

The postcolonial critique has also not yet reached all artists, meaning that they too can be rightly judged for failing to resist the exploitation of certain stories and their protagonists. In other cases, stories emerge that neither succeed aesthetically nor effectively reckon with the human rights situation. But despite all short-term or media successes, art should not be simply put "into service." Art has the power to create a space beyond the superficially visible and beyond interpretation. Art is the contingency of form and thus (also) of social possibilities. Within it, emotions and experiences—as well as insights and dreams—can find a place. By means of the associative—of collage, of flashbacks, of flashforwards, of superimposing and merging people, of themes and events from different epochs and regions—more complex situations can be processed. The perception of the possible can be projected far into utopian space through the artistic processing of human rights material.

First Conclusions

In the prison of the everyday, we too seldom lift our eyes, too seldom shift our gaze from the close-up to the wide panoramic view and back again. We do not question ourselves and everything around us often enough. Do we lack the time to sustain the presence of mind necessary to grasp all the contradictions and ambivalences within the struggle for human rights and human life itself? I don't even know how to answer this question for myself. For now, I only hold myself to the minimum standard: I am making an effort.

If some passages here should read apodictically or like calls to action, they are rather intended as invitations to think, to discuss and, of course, to commit oneself to the struggle for one's own rights—for example, against mass surveillance or the right to health, or for those living next door, those in prisons, old people's homes and refugee facilities, but also for people far away, in global solidarity.

These days, it has not always been easy for me to write a text that is carried by a Gramscian "optimism of the will," which in turn, according to Ernst Bloch, can only be justified as "militant optimism." It helps to realize that failure is inevitable in the effort to make this world a good one. Nevertheless, such a commitment is imperative.

I also feel an even stronger sense of obligation when I realize that many of those whose thoughts I refer to here, from Gramsci to Benjamin to Hirschman, from Adorno to Bloch, have indeed experienced darker times than we have. My friends in Argentina, Mexico, and India have also lived and worked under much more difficult conditions.

And who actually is the "we" that I occasionally invoke here? Is there a "we" at all? Sometimes, I am unsure of this myself. At times, I refer to the "we" of human rights lawyers or those organized within the human rights movement. But with this "we," I want to address all people who stand in solidarity with others whenever human rights are at stake.

But how do we actually organize encounters, conversations, and discussions during these difficult times? How do we keep ourselves from feeling alone and from looking to escape these difficult realities? Only those who can answer these questions for themselves will be able to help others.

In the end, one thing is absolutely clear for me: maintaining the energy, empathy, and courage necessary for these struggles for truth and justice, especially during these times, is not possible without friendship, without a desire for human encounters, without love and joy in life. In this way, we can then face Zygmunt Bauman's plea to make the angel of history turn around: "More than at any other time, we—human inhabitants of the Earth—are in the either/or situation: we face joining either hands, or common graves.

Acknowledgments

For their support in this endeavor, I thank Chris Dertinger and Annette Hulek, Rieke Ernst, Markus Beeko, Andreas Fischer-Lescano and Carsten Gericke, Bernd Müssig, Erwin Single and Peter Seibert, as well as Alfio Furnari and Matthias Landwehr from my agency Landwehr and Alexander Roesler and Yelenah Frahm from Fischer Verlag. For their support for the English version, I would like to thank Joshua Castellino, David Youssef, Josh Mailman, and Colin Robinson and his team from OR Books.

Further reading

For those who would like to follow up on any of the references in my text, I recommend the following reading.

Zygmunt Bauman's *Retrotopia* (Berlin 2017) and Enzo Traverso's *Left Melancholy–On the Strength of a Hidden Tradition* (Münster 2019) take up Walter Benjamin's historical-philosophical theses.

On concrete utopias, Alexander Neupert-Doppler offers a nice overview as editor of the small volume *Konkrete Utopien* [Concrete Utopias] (Stuttgart 2018). Felwine Sarr also takes up Ernst Bloch's topos in *Afrotopia* (Berlin 2019). Sociologist Hellmut Wilke provides a good explanation of the concept of intervention in *Systems Theory II: Intervention Theory* (Stuttgart 1994).

Lynn Hunt, in *Inventing Human Rights – A History* (New York 2007), deals primarily with the French Revolution. An inspiring essay on the Haitian Revolution was written by Michel-Rolph Trouillot, "An Unthinkable History," in the superb exhibition catalog of the Black Atlantic (Berlin 2004), in which Paul Gilroy also explains the concept behind the catalog's title and Susan Buck-Morss elucidates her theses on Hegel and Haiti.

The anthology *Die Revolution der Menschenrechte* [The Revolution of Human Rights] (Berlin 2011), edited by Christoph Menke and Franceska Raimondi, plays a central role in my reflections. Jan Eckel's *Die Ambivalenz des Guten—Menschenrechte in der internationalen Politik seit den 1940er Jahren* [The Ambivalence of Good: Human Rights in International Politics since the 1940s] (Göttingen 2014) not only describes institutional human rights policy since the 1940s, especially the period around the 1948 Universal Declaration of Human Rights, but also analyzes Amnesty International and the "reinvention of Western human rights activism" with the help of numerous internal documents. The genesis of the human rights system after 1945 is analyzed by Fabian Klose in *Menschenrechte im Schatten kolonialer Gewalt—Die Dekolonisierungskriege in Kenia und Algerien 1945 bis 1962* [Human Rights in the Shadow of Colonial Violence: The Decolonization Wars in Kenya and Algeria from 1945 to 1962] (Munich 2009) and Roland Burke in *Decolonization and the Evolution of International Human Rights* (Philadelphia 2010) from the perspective of decolonization. Important texts concerning decolonial legal theory have been presented for the first time in German by Karina Theurer and myself as editors in *Dekoloniale Rechtskritik und Rechtspraxis* [Decolonial Legal Critique and Legal Practice] (Baden-Baden 2020). Tshepo Madlingozi published a very clear text in "On Transitional Justice Entrepreneurs and the Production of Victims" in the *Journal of Human Rights Practice* in 2010.

A vast number of books deal with the (current) crisis situation and resistance movements. I found Keeanga-Yamahtta Taylor's *From Black Lives Matter to Black Liberation* (Münster 2017) very instructive, as well as her work on the more recent feminist movement *8M—The Great Feminist Strike: Constellations of March 8* (Vienna 2018—available for download online).

For those who want to learn more about the legal cases addressed here, the website of my organization, the European Center for Constitutional and Human Rights (ECCHR)—www.ecchr.eu—provides summaries and explanations. Those who want to get down to hard economic realities should read Katharina Pistor: *The Code of Capital: How Law Creates Wealth and Inequality*.

Samuel Moyn has provided a recent history of human rights in *The Last Utopia* (Boston 2010), and currently critiques developments in *Human Rights in an Unequal World* (Boston 2018) as strongly as Stephen Hopgood in *The Endtimes of Human Rights* (New York 2013). The theses of the two provoked a controversial debate that can be traced, among others, in "Debating the Endtimes of Human Rights" (Amsterdam 2014—available online) and especially in Kathryn Sikkink's *Evidence for Hope in Human Rights Work in the 21st Century* (Princeton 2017).

On the subject of art and human rights, countless recommendations can be made. The exhibition catalogs *Forensis* (Berlin 2014), *Everyday Life and Forgetting: Argentina*

1976 to 2003 (Berlin 2003), and *Ex Argentina. Schritte zur Flucht von der Arbeit zum Tun* [Ex Argentina: Steps to Escape from Work to Action] (Cologne 2004), as well as Milo Rau's *Congo Tribunal* (Berlin 2017) may suffice as examples here—and those who have not yet read it should definitely pick up Susan Sontag's *Das Leiden anderer betrachten* [Regarding the Pain of Others] (Munich 2003).

Wolfgang Kaleck is the founder and General Secretary of the European Center for Constitutional and Human Rights (ECCHR) in Berlin. Working with partners around the world, ECCHR takes legal proceedings against individuals, corporations, and state actors who have breached the law relating to human rights.

Printed in the USA
CPSIA information can be obtained
at www.ICGtesting.com
JSHW022315100124
55228JS00002B/5